ORDNANCE SURVEY LEISURE GUIDE

DAYS OUT
FROM
LONDON

▲ Mill End, Hambleden

AA | O↑S

Produced jointly by the Publishing Division of
The Automobile Association and the Ordnance Survey

Editorial contributors: Richard Cavendish (The Natural Setting, London and its Countryside, People and Places, A House in the Country, Pubs and Inns, The Capital City and boxed features); Leigh Hatts (Walks); Rebecca Snelling (Fact File, Tours); Peter Wenham (Gazetteer); Hugh Westacott (Tours and Walks).

Original photography: Derek Forss and Malc Birkitt

Phototypeset by Wyvern Typesetting, Bristol
Colour separation by LC Repro & Sons Ltd, Aldermaston
Printed and bound by William Clowes Limited, Beccles and London

Maps extracted from The Automobile Association 1:200 000 and 1:300 000 Automaps database © The Automobile Association; and the Ordnance Survey 1:250 000 Routemaster Series enlarged to 1:190 080, and 1:25 000 Pathfinder Series with the permission of Her Majesty's Stationery Office. Crown copyright.

Additions to the maps by the Cartographic Department of The Automobile Association and the Ordnance Survey.

Produced by the Publishing Division of The Automobile Association.

Distributed in the United Kingdom by the Ordnance Survey, Southampton, and the Publishing Division of The Automobile Association, Fanum House, Basingstoke, Hampshire RG21 2EA.

First edition 1992

AA ISBN 0 7495 0370 X
OS ISBN 0 319 00284 5

Published by The Automobile Association and the Ordnance Survey.

Introduction: Hatfield Forest

Contents

▲ The Pantiles, Tunbridge Wells

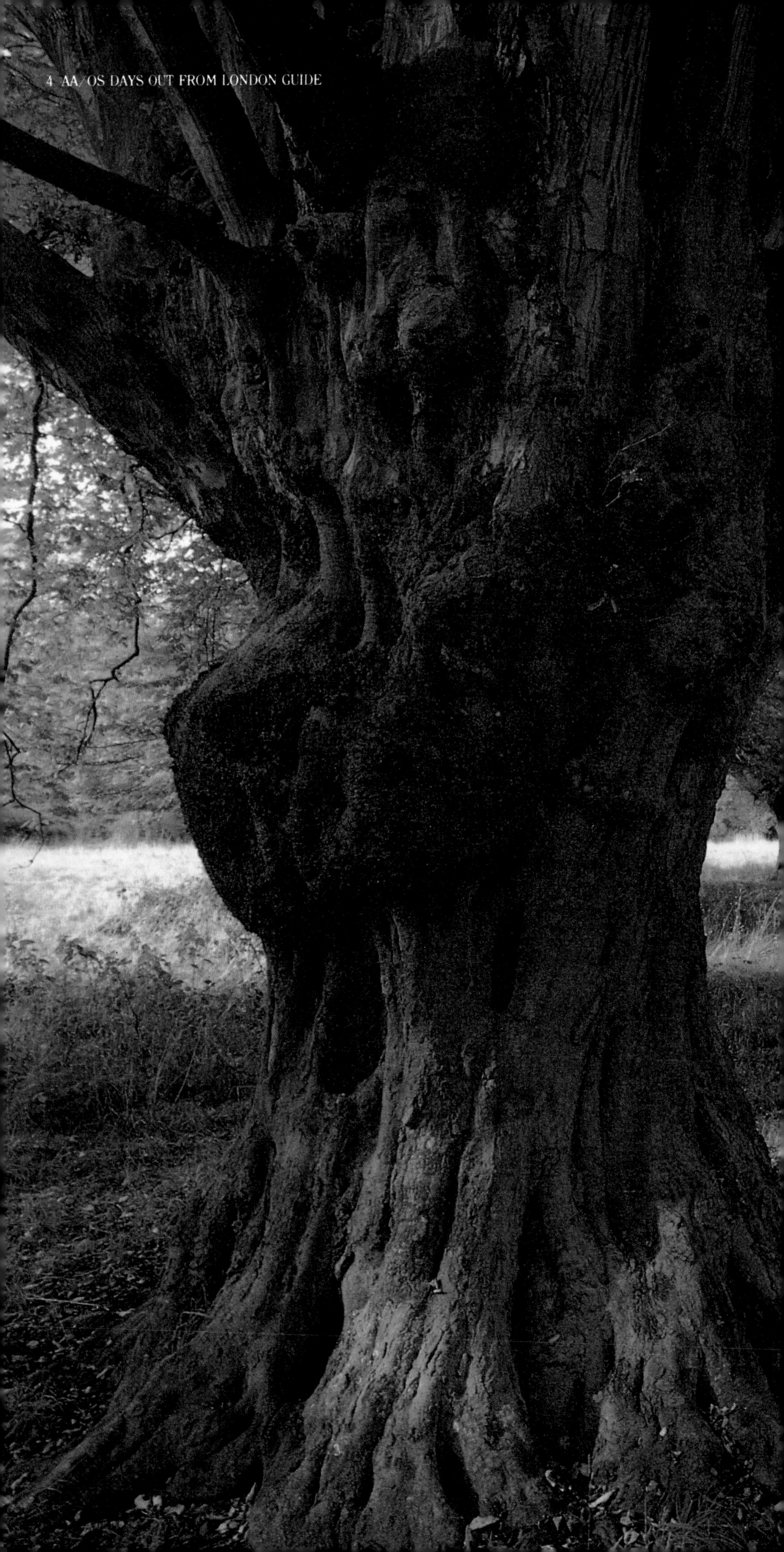

Introduction

Over the centuries London has grown ever larger, but within easy reach of the capital there remains a wide variety of beautiful scenery, from the Chiltern Hills to the North Downs, from the Thames valley to the Thames estuary. Lying in this countryside are historic towns and picturesque villages, glorious castles and sumptuous stately homes, world-famous gardens and traditional pubs, exotic wildlife collections and sensational theme parks. Whether you are searching for the solitude of a hill walk or the bustle of a market town, this guide provides the answer. It explores the history, traditions, geology and wildlife and describes the towns, villages and hamlets of the London area; walks and motor tours seek out the hidden corners and the finest landscapes. Written entirely by people who live and work in the region, backed by the AA's research expertise and the Ordnance Survey's mapping, this guide is equally useful to the visitor and to the resident of London's environs.

The Natural Setting

Two chalk hill ranges, the Chilterns and the North Downs, dominate the geography of the area around London. They are set at an angle to each other, like the jaws of an open pair of nutcrackers, with the hinge to the west. Between the jaws lies the flat clay of the London Basin, with London itself at the heart of the nut. The countryside around the city's perimeter forms the Green Belt and is to some extent protected against development. Flowing across the central basin, through London and out to the North Sea, is the Thames, and the whole area is drained by this great river and its tributaries.

Grassland, Downs and Beechwoods

North-west of the Chilterns lies the prosperous farming country of the Vale of Aylesbury, whose lush grassland has for centuries nourished dairy herds and fattened beef cattle, sheep and poultry to feed hungry Londoners. The 300-acre Great Field at Creslow, near Whitchurch, is England's biggest single pasture. Cattle have grazed on it since Elizabethan times, and well down into this century the Vale was famous for the rearing of Aylesbury ducks.

There are fine views over the Vale from the steep chalk scarp of the Chilterns. The range runs for 50 miles or so, from the Thames at the Goring Gap in Oxfordshire, north-east across Buckinghamshire to peter out north of Luton in Bedfordshire. Along the crest runs a long-distance trail, the Ridgeway Path.

The highest points cluster in the stretch between Watlington and Tring. Watlington Hill is one of a string of National Trust properties along the range, with a forest of yew and whitebeam, dogwood, hawthorn and the romantically named wayfaring tree. Further north-east is Pulpit Wood with its prehistoric hill-fort, and Ivinghoe Beacon has another hill-fort. Coombe Hill, near Wendover, is the highest viewpoint in the Chilterns at 852ft.

The wind chases cloud shadows across the short, springy turf of the downland. At Dunstable Downs five Bronze Age bell-barrows preside over wild flowers with entrancing names like eyebright and fairy flag, while kestrels and skylarks hover overhead. So do the gliders which take off here.

The Chilterns are much better known, however, for the magnificent beechwoods at such beauty spots as Wendover Woods, Bradenham Woods and Burnham Beeches. The beech may have given Buckinghamshire its name (from Old English *bece*) and beechwoods supported the traditional Chilterns furniture industry. The tree thrives on thin dry soil, growing 100ft-high or more. Little will grow in its heavy shade and beechwoods are softly carpeted by brown leaves and lit by gleams of dappled sunlight. Fallow and muntjac deer wander among the trees, dragonflies dart and hover above ponds, and there are grey squirrels and foxes, woodpeckers and owls, collared doves and a lively variety of snails. The National Trust's Ashridge estate, north of Tring, is home to a rarity – the edible dormouse, *glis glis*.

The Chilterns chalk is mixed with flint, of which many of the Chilterns churches are built. Chalk soaks up rain rapidly and the lack of surface water and natural springs in the area explain why it was thinly settled until comparatively recently. For centuries it was bandit country.

From the scarp the lie of the land slopes gently to the south-east, down towards London, whose need for milk and meat supports dairy farming and the rearing of pigs and poultry. The valleys run south-eastwards. Many of them are dry, but a few streams like the Wye, the Misbourne and the Chess run south to the Thames.

All the main road and rail routes follow this north-west/south-east orientation into and out of London. The A41 road from London to Aylesbury follows the course of a Roman road, Akeman Street. The main line from Euston to Birmingham and the north-west takes the same route initially, along the valley of the Gade and the Bulbourne, past Hemel Hempstead, Berkhamsted and Tring. It keeps close company with the Grand Union Canal to Birmingham, constructed in the 1790s as the Grand Junction Canal. North of Tring the canal reservoirs nourish reeds and bullrushes and multitudes of water birds. Other roads and railway lines use gaps in the Chilterns at Wendover, Princes Risborough and High Wycombe.

England Meditative

Eastwards from the Chilterns lies gently undulating country in Hertfordshire and western Essex – a landscape of low hills and green slopes, summer cornfields and plenty of trees. Narrow lanes thread the fields and hedgerows to villages nestling round greens in what E M Forster described as 'England at its quietest, England meditative'.

Churches and grand houses were built of flint or imported stone. With no local stone to build a steeple, the little flint churches often have a

Views from Whiteleaf Hill on the Chilterns escarpment stretch across the Vale of Aylesbury ▼

'Hertfordshire spike' – a diminutive spirelet of lead. From Tudor times on, local brick and tiles were increasingly used for building. Though there is still plenty of pleasant countryside, the area's character is under constant threat from London commuting and bigger and better roads.

There is far more surface water here than on the Chilterns, more springs, lakes and rivers. The Lea (or Lee) rises in Bedfordshire at Leagrave and runs south through Luton, Hatfield and Hertford on course for the Thames east of the Isle of Dogs. At Hertford the Lea is joined by delightfully named tributaries – the Mimram, the Rib and the Beane. South of Waltham Abbey are huge reservoirs of water for London.

East of Bishop's Stortford the nightingales sing and fallow deer graze among the pollarded hornbeams of Hatfield Forest. Wild orchids grow in the marshes near the lake and there are silver birch coppices and wide expanses of open grassland. Further south, Epping Forest is another remnant of the hunting forest that once covered most of Essex. Further south still is the Thames estuary.

The Thames
The Thames enters the area from the west, skirting the Chilterns past Henley and Marlow before turning south for Cookham, Maidenhead and Windsor, to go on to Staines and into Greater London. The recently created Thames Path is based on the old towpath, used by horses and gangs of men hauling heavily loaded barges in the 18th and early 19th centuries, when the river was still a commercial highway of the first importance: before the coming of railways and motor transport. It is quite unlike the other long-distance paths, which traverse high country or coastline. The walk along the Thames goes through lush lowlands, stocked with meadows and gardens, prosperous villages and small towns. Launches, cruisers, punts and rowing boats swarm on the water; walkers, joggers and cyclists on the banks, while anglers contemplate the passing stream. Among the teeming wildlife are numerous river birds – swans, herons, ducks, kingfishers.

There is a wealth of buildings

▲ The look-out at Box Hill on the North Downs.

to be enjoyed along the way too, from churches and stately homes to stockbroker's palaces, riverside villas and bungalows with lawns running down to the water, mills and boatyards, waterside inns, locks, weirs and bridges.

At Windsor the river glides past the castle, home of English kings and queens since William the Conqueror. At Runnymede King John signed Magna Carta. The London Stone at Staines marks the highest point at which the river is affected by the tide, and so the beginning of the City of London's jurisdiction over the water. The Lord Mayor used to be rowed solemnly downstream from here in his stately barge on an annual inspection of the river. Huge reservoirs in this area include the Queen Mary Reservoir, which is twice the size of Hyde Park.

The Thames flows on along its historic course past Hampton Court and Kew Gardens, and through the centre of London past the Houses of Parliament and the Tower. Beyond Tower Bridge lies what was once the busy port of London and the new developments of Docklands, before the river reaches its broad estuary between the tidal flats and mudbanks along the shorelines of Essex and Kent.

In the South
To the south of Greater London the chalk reappears again as the North Downs. Running across the middle of Surrey and into Kent, the range forms something of a mirror image to the Chilterns, though more heavily built over. Well wooded with beech and yew, the gentle slope is on the northern side, towards London. The steep scarp is on the southern edge. At the western end the range narrows down to the thin spine of the Hog's Back running between Guildford and Farnham.

Roads and railways fan out from London to the south through the North Downs valleys and the rivers here run north to the Thames. At the eastern end of the Downs the Medway rises near Edenbridge and after wandering through the meadows at Tonbridge carves its way through the chalk to reach its estuary beyond Rochester. Further west, the Darent – 'in whose waters clean', wrote

Maidstone, the sandstone contains layers of limestone. Known as Kentish ragstone, this is good building stone and Boughton Monchelsea Place, near Maidstone, is a handsome example of it. It was used for the Tower of London as well.

At the other end, on the borders of Berkshire, Hampshire and Surrey, the sandy, acid soil is of little use for farming and supports broad stretches of heath, covered with gorse, heather and bracken, with pinewoods and stands of silver birch. Bagshot Heath was once notorious for highwaymen. Some of this land is used for military training in the Aldershot area. To the south, near Hindhead, is the spectacular Devil's Punch Bowl. These areas are rich in wildlife and plants, with a great variety of ferns, mosses, fungi and lichens. There are grass snakes, nightjars and woodcocks here and such rarities as the sand lizard and the Dartford warbler. Surrey has more trees per acre than any other county in England, and as most of the shire is in the Green Belt and

the National Trust is a major landowner, substantial areas are open to the public and there is still plenty of broadleaved woodland.

Across southern Surrey, northern Sussex and western Kent lies a broad band of Weald clay. This is prosperous farming country, where beef and dairy cattle and sheep graze the pastures in a landscape of handsome farmhouses and barns, idyllic villages, orchards, ponds and sparkling streams, woods and rich hedgerows. Here again are great houses: Knole, Penshurst Place, Clandon Park to name only a few.

The old North Downs churches are built of flint, sometimes mixed with chalk rubble. South of the Downs there are many half-timbered buildings to be seen, but the main construction material is brick, made of the local clay and used for churches as well as houses of all sizes. Local tiles were used, too, for walls as well as roofs. Sadly, this whole area is under great pressure from demand for new housing and faster road and rail routes.

Spenser, 'ten thousand fishes play' – rises at Westerham in Kent and goes through a break in the North Downs at Otford to Darenth and Dartford, reaching the Thames east of Erith.

The River Mole has diligently cut a steep cliff north of Dorking at the popular beauty spot of Box Hill. It loops its way past the sumptuous 18th-century landscape garden at Painshill Park to the Thames near Hampton Court. The Wey rises on the Surrey/Hampshire border and flows through Guildford to the Thames north of Weybridge. Stretches of canal were built along it in the 17th and 18th centuries and the Wey Navigation is now popular for pleasure boating.

Lying to the south of the North Downs and parallel to them is the Lower Greensand Ridge, which rises to 965ft at Leith Hill, the highest point in the south-east of England. The views on a clear day extend to the English Channel in one direction and St Paul's Cathedral in the other. The bluebell woods here are famous and there are splendid beeches, rhododendrons and oaks.

At the eastern end of the Greensand, near Sevenoaks and

Epping Forest, on London's doorstep, is a timeless ancient woodland ▼

London and its Countryside

▲ Until the 19th century many of London's 'suburbs' were a day or so's journey from the capital. Today's view from Richmond Hill (top) is still relatively rural, but Edgware has changed beyond all recognition since this 1858 sketch

Within 20 or 30 miles of London lies some of England's most attractive countryside. It survives in spite of the city, and yet also because of it. Underlying the history and character of the area is the tension between the countryside and the dominating city which lies at its centre like a giant spider in its web. London constantly threatens to engulf and spoil the countryside, but on the other hand London supplies the market and the money to keep the farms and nursery gardens going, the entrancing villages spick and span, and the countryside in pleasing shape.

As London prospered and its population grew, it began to spread out from its two early focal points – the City and Westminster – and swallow up the villages outside. Until well into the 19th century, however, places like Richmond and Camberwell, Streatham and Islington, still enjoyed a separate existence. Although heavily dependent on London, they were not yet physically part of it. The major factor in ending this state of affairs was the coming of the railways.

London's Villages

Richmond was originally a fishing hamlet on the Thames, eight miles or so from Westminster. It turned into a smart satellite of London society from about 1500, when Henry VII rebuilt the old manor house as a palace. Little is left of the palace today, but it stood close to Richmond Green and the Old Deer Park was originally its garden and park. The Tudors loved Richmond and spent much time there, which meant that courtiers and their households spent much time

air of smartness and sophistication that the royal court originally conferred on it.

To the south-east, long before lawn tennis was invented, Wimbledon developed as a village on the high ground to the south of Putney Heath and Wimbledon Common, where, in the 18th century, highwaymen lurked in wait for coaches and travellers on the Portsmouth road. When the railway came through in 1838, it kept to the low ground to the south of the village. Gradually terraces of houses began to go up close to the railway station and Wimbledon's centre of gravity eventually shifted there, though most of the residential streets were not laid out until the 1880s.

Streatham in the 18th century was a farming village among the fields halfway between London and the country town of Croydon. The discovery of a healthful spring in 1659 had created a small spa. In 1841 the population was about 6,000. Three railway stations opened in the 1850s and '60s, and by the end of the century the population had swelled to 70,000. Some fields and woods were still left, but in the 1920s the whole area was covered with a warren of small houses.

When Queen Victoria came to the throne, even a place as close to London as Camberwell was still a village, whose green fields and ripening orchards sheltered the Camberwell beauty butterfly. Mendelssohn wrote his lyrical *Spring Song* there in 1842, and the traditional country fair on Camberwell Green survived until 1855. By then the houses had spread along the main roads and Camberwell's beauty was doomed.

Equally close in, to the north of London, Islington was still a rustic spot when the 19th century dawned. Dairy farms supplied Londoners' fresh milk and nursery gardens grew their vegetables. Huge herds of cattle, sheep and pigs were driven bellowing, bleating and grunting down from the north to Smithfield market, feeding on Islington's nourishing pastures on the way. Between 1801 and 1901 all this changed as the population exploded from 10,000 to 335,000 and green pastures were covered with slum tenements and gin palaces.

Further north, the sleepy villages of Upper and Lower Edmonton stood peacefully on the road to Hertford. Better-off Londoners liked to drive out to the Bell at Edmonton for a country day-out. In 1872, however, the railway line from Liverpool Street brought a tidal wave of East End workers and their families. In Finchley the area west of the Great North Road was described as 'rural' in 1876, while rustic Edgware stayed comparatively unspoiled until the tube line from Charing Cross arrived in 1924.

Wild Country

Some areas further outside London were wild and dangerous country for surprisingly long. The deep Chilterns woods sheltered outlaws and robbers for centuries and the Steward of the Chiltern Hundreds – whose sinecure office is now applied for by a Member of Parliament who wants to resign his seat – originally had the real and ungrateful task of keeping order. Hindhead in Surrey in the 18th century was a notorious haunt of highwaymen and rogues lurking along the London to Portsmouth road (now the A3), and there was a gibbet to hang them on. On the heathland and deep in the Devil's Punch Bowl, left prudently alone by the respectable classes, lived the Broom Squires, a rough and ready folk who supported themselves by broom-making, charcoal-burning, poaching and thieving.

At the end of the 18th century smuggling was still flourishing in the area south of Dorking, around the Holmwoods and Ewhurst. Contraband from the Continent was brought up from Sussex at night by strings of packhorses, to be hidden until it could be sent on to London, and there are still cottages in this part of the county which have capacious cellars for concealing smuggled bales and barrels.

As late as the 1880s there were remote Surrey villages where local rascals still paid for their misdeeds by being pelted in the stocks.

A Two-Way Street

Hertfordshire was always known – and still is – for its pure and bracing air. A writer in 1700 said that the air in the neighbourhood of Flamstead,

there too, which in turn meant that a sizeable village grew up to house them and supply their needs. The Green, where the villagers normally pastured their sheep, echoed to the clash and thunder of jousting tournaments, later to be more peaceably replaced by cricket matches.

The 18th century saw handsome houses going up on Richmond Hill, with its sweeping view over the Thames. Sir Joshua Reynolds had a house there and painted the prospect. Londoners came to take the waters at Richmond Wells on the hill and the stars of the London stage played at the Richmond theatre. The population grew big enough to need a bridge over the Thames, a charmingly civilised structure completed in 1777.

In 1840 the railway arrived. In its wake it drew prosperous Victorian business and professional men and their families. Today's Richmond boasts elegant houses and cottages of the 18th and 19th centuries and still retains the between Hemel Hempstead and Luton, was so invigorating that an old woman of the village had lived to be 120, while the meanest curs from there could outrun the swiftest greyhounds bred anywhere else. By the same token, as another Hertfordshire writer pointed out in 1704, 'The rich Soil and wholesome Air, and the excellence of the County, have drawn hither the Wealthiest Citizens of London'.

Moneyed Londoners bought estates outside the city, settled themselves down as squires and gentlefolk, and became stout guardians and preservers of country ways. At the same time, families based in the countryside earned a living, and sometimes wealth and eminence, as suppliers to the London market. George Evelyn made his money out of gunpowder mills at Long Ditton and Wootton in Surrey. His grandson was John Evelyn, the 17th-century diarist and a founder member of the Royal Society, who inherited a substantial estate and lived and died at Wootton House (now a training college). John Evelyn loved pine trees and the pinewoods which stretch from Wotton to Leith Hill today are descended from his plantings.

It was London demand which made Kent 'the garden of England', with its orchards, hop fields and picturesque oast-houses. Areas near the capital with sandy soil – which warms up quickly in the spring and produces an early crop – proved ideal for market gardening to supply the London appetite for fresh vegetables and flowers. Acres of tomatoes have ripened under glass in the Lea valley, south of Hertford, to stock London grocery counters. Bagshot, Windlesham, Chobham and Woking in Surrey, where the soil favours rhododendrons, azaleas and heathers, are known for nursery gardens.

The relationship between London and its countryside has always been a two-way street. In the 18th century wagons creaked and trundled out of London into the Hertfordshire lanes every day. They were laden with London dung to be spread on the fields as manure – night soil, horse droppings, chimney soot, ashes, rags. The city's debris was used to nourish the soil that fed it.

A Day in the Country
In 1822 the choleric, Surrey-born William Cobbet, author of *Rural Rides*, travelled north through Barnet and Potter's Bar on his way to Cambridgeshire. He noted irritably that, 'the enormous *Wen*', as he called London, 'has swelled out to the distance of six or seven miles'.

London was steadily spreading not only its debris over the surrounding countryside, but its people and houses as well. Again, it was the arrival of the railways, from the late 1830s, which really opened the area outside London up to large numbers of Londoners, as settlers and also as holiday-makers and day-trippers. London businessmen took to going out for a day's shooting in Hertfordshire. Victorian ramblers would take the train to a rural station and explore the nearby country on foot, assisted by the much improved large-scale maps of the period. A London club known as the Sunday Tramps used to take regular days out in the Surrey countryside. One of the founders of this group was Leslie Stephenson, 'the patron saint of ramblers', who knew the area between Guildford, Leatherhead and Leith Hill like the back of his hand. Buried in Godstone churchyard is Edmund Seybang Taylor, who wrote rambling guides under the pseudonym of 'Walker Miles'.

Hot on the heels of the walkers came the cyclists. The first velocipedes, or 'boneshakers', appeared in the 1860s. Cycling clubs were soon formed and the first organised bicycling tour on record in England set out from London in

1873 and passed through Hertfordshire by Potters Bar, Welwyn and Stevenage, before vanishing towards the frozen north. By 1880 there were more than 200 touring cycle clubs in Britain and in the Edwardian era suburban cyclists would whirr and pedal along the country roads in swooping and whirling flocks, the men in knickerbockers and heavy shoes, the girls in bloomers, belted jackets and straw hats.

The introduction of bank holidays in 1871 had multiplied the numbers of Londoners setting cheerfully out for a day in the country. Thousands of East Enders used to take the bank holiday trains to the pleasure gardens at Rye House, near Hoddesden on the

Hertfordshire border: not entirely to the peace of mind of the local inhabitants, who complained of too much drunkenness and loutishness.

Places along the Thames, too, played host to growing numbers of trippers out from the capital for a day's fun on the river in a punt or a rowing boat – or for longer river holidays, whose perils humorously retold made Jerome K Jerome's *Three Men in a Boat* a hit in 1889. Riverside towns like Marlow, Maidenhead and Henley began to grow as Londoners moved in to settle, and all along its banks the river sprouted Victorian and Edwardian mansions with smoothly shaven lawns, tennis courts and boathouses.

Garden City and Green Belt
The speed of railway travel made it possible for the first time for large numbers of Londoners to combine working in the city with living in the country. The difficulty, of course, was that it ceased to be country as more and more people moved into it. Between 1801 and 1901 the population of what is now the Greater London area increased sixfold, from a little over a million to about 6½ million. By 1939 it was 8½ million. A tide of suburban housing estates crawled relentlessly across open country, covering fields and pastures, woods and heaths with a mass of streets, *bijou* residences, back gardens, shops, churches, restaurants, pubs, bowling greens and tennis clubs.

New towns were created directly by the railways. Woking, now one of Surrey's principal commercial centres, grew up after 1838 around the railway station, which was a mile or two outside the original village of Old Woking. Redhill was an inconspicuous hamlet until the London-to-Brighton line came by in 1841 and set off its expansion into a commuter town. In Kent, Tonbridge grew rapidly in the 19th century as a railway junction.

The areas most heavily suburbanised were naturally those closest to London. In Buckinghamshire it was the southern stretch of the county, roughly from Beaconsfield and Gerrards Cross down to Slough. The Metropolitan Railway, which opened London's first underground railway in 1863, built an overground extension from Baker Street north-west to Harrow, and later extended it into the Chilterns, to Rickmansworth, Amersham and Chesham, which became dormitory towns for London commuters. Equally affected were the southern belt of Hertfordshire, western Essex and the northern slope of the North Downs in Surrey and Kent.

The intellectuals' tendency to sneer at suburbs overlooks the fact that they provide the most popular style of living ever devised in Britain and are on all counts preferable to urban slums. By 1900, however, Cobbett's 'enormous Wen' was devouring its surrounding countryside at such a rate as to cause serious alarm.

One of the suggested solutions came from Ebenezer Howard,

Days gone by . . . crowds enjoying a bank holiday on Hampstead Heath ▼

the visionary author of *Tomorrow* (1898), who advocated 'the garden city': by which he meant a city in a garden, not a city of gardens. The plan was to build outside London brand-new cities of strictly limited size, set in pleasant countryside from which the city population would draw spiritual and moral refreshment. Each city would be self-sufficient. The inhabitants would work there as well as live there. The first one was built at Letchworth in Hertfordshire in 1905. After World War I, Howard formed a company to build Welwyn Garden City in the countryside north of Hatfield, some 30 miles from London. The principal architect was a Frenchman, Louis de Soissons.

The new city was planned with curving, tree-lined avenues, a separate industrial zone and a shopping and civic area, surrounded by groups of houses in a pleasant neo-Georgian style. It had its own schools, churches and cottage hospital. The earliest inhabitants were unkindly caricatured as earnest, bearded vegetarians and teetotallers, clad in homespun tweeds and sandals, but Welwyn Garden City attracted 10,000 residents in its first dozen years. Attracting industrial firms proved much more dificult, and though some did eventually settle in – the leading employer was a cereal factory making shredded wheat – many of the residents have always commuted to London to work.

Ebenezer Howard was also a proponent of fastening round London a 'green belt' of farmland and open countryside protected against further development. This would forcibly prevent London from spreading any further and would again function as a much-needed reservoir of country recreation and refreshment for Londoners. It would also save independent towns and villages outside London from blending into each other in an amorphous mass.

The idea slowly gained ground. The London County Council began to move in this direction in the 1930s and today's Green Belt is mainly a creation of the period after World War II. By the 1970s it extended in the north out to the Vale of Aylesbury and almost to the towns of Hatfield, Harlow and Basildon. On the west it included Windsor and from there covered most of Surrey and stretched into Kent beyond Sevenoaks and Dartford. Protected status, however, did not prevent the M25 motorway being built through the Green Belt in the 1980s.

Another attempt to establish self-sufficient communities outside London came after 1945 with the creation of the New Towns. They include Bracknell, Hemel Hempstead, Hatfield, Stevenage, Harlow, Basildon and Crawley. Unfortunately, these new developments were carried out at a time when architecture and town planning in Britain were at a low ebb and they have been fiercely criticised for the ugliness and monotony of their concrete architecture, the gracelessness of their identical shopping precincts and their lack of any individuality or separate identity. Certainly they have not solved the perennial problem of London and its threatened countryside.

Going to Greenwich on an Easter Monday in the mid-19th century ▼

A House in the Country

▲ Mentmore Towers was built as a country home for the Rothschilds ▼

Queen Victoria's reign witnessed an invasion of Buckinghamshire and Hertfordshire by the Rothschilds. Amply equipped with money, intelligence, taste and charm, these banking grandees built themselves palatial houses in the Home Counties and settled as to the manner born into country society and its pattern of hunting, shooting and fishing, huge weekend house parties and glamorous balls.

Mentmore Towers, a colossal pile in fake Jacobean, was built in the 1850s for Mayer Amschel de Rothschild, who, while he was about it, rebuilt the village of Mentmore as well. The big house had central heating and artificial ventilation throughout. Leopold Rothschild bought Ascott Hall, near Wing, and enlarged it. Another branch installed themselves at Tring Park, where the second Lord Rothschild kept a private menagerie of wild animals in the grounds. He liked to drive

through Tring in a carriage drawn by zebras.

Most magical of all is Waddesdon Manor, an imitation French château built for Ferdinand de Rothschild in the 1870s and big enough to house 100 evacuees in World War II. A whole army of labourers was enlisted to build the house and park, construct roads and lay 7 miles of water pipes. Full-grown trees with huge balls of earth packed round their roots were dragged laboriously across country on wagons hauled by 16 carthorses apiece, to be planted in the grounds, which were beautified with elaborate fountains and a rococo aviary.

Astonishingly lavish as their scale of operations was, the Rothschilds were only the latest in a long line of the rich and powerful who had built themselves country retreats.

Bishops and Courtiers

Already by Tudor times the area within 30 miles or so of London was a convenient location for the country residences of royalty, courtiers, bishops and businessmen. The bishops of London had a half-timbered palace at Much Hadham in Hertfordshire, as a retreat from the pastoral and political cares of the capital. Cased in brick in the 17th century, it still survives after being used as a girls' school and a lunatic asylum. The bishops of Ely built the Old Palace at Hatfield, which was appropriated by Henry VIII. Part of it survives in the grounds of the gigantic Jacobean mansion of the Cecils.

Henry VIII demanded Knole, outside Sevenoaks in Kent, from Archbishop Cranmer and substantially enlarged it. Standing on a knoll (hence its name) in a spacious deer park, the house had been used by the archbishops of Canterbury for 80 years. The king also seized Hever Castle in Kent, the girlhood home of his executed second wife, Anne Boleyn. The Boleyns were a courtier family, whose fortune had originally been made in business in London by Anne's great-grandfather.

Not far from Hever, Ightham Mote, set among woods and

guarded by its moat, is a marvellously preserved example of a country house of the period. At the core is the medieval great hall, where the household lived, ate and slept in a boisterous tumult. Smoke from the hearth curled up among the rafters and out through the roof, while the hunting dogs scratched for fleas and gnawed their bones on the rush-strewn floor. The house was bought in 1521 by a Tudor civil servant, Richard Clement, and later in the century passed to the Selby family, who would own it for close on 300 years.

Sir Richard Weston was courtier, friend and faithful servant to Henry VIII, who rewarded him with the manor of Sutton, near Guildford. He built Sutton Place there in time for a royal visit in 1533. A career at court was highly lucrative, but could also be highly dangerous. Sir Richard's son, Francis, a notable tennis player, was caught up in the Anne Boleyn imbroglio and accused of being one of her lovers. He was executed in 1536, but this embarrassing episode did the family no damage in the long run.

Sir Richard's house was built in brick with terracotta ornamentation, ranged round a courtyard. One of the terracotta details is a panel of 12 winged cherubs, and above them are barrels, or 'tuns', punning on the family name. The north side and the gatehouse were pulled down in the 18th century, but otherwise the house is much as it was, though the interior has been altered many times. The Weston direct line died out in 1782. In 1959 the house was acquired by J Paul Getty, the oil magnate, whose most trumpeted innovation was the installation of pay telephones.

Other Tudor mansions close to London include Dorney Court, near Windsor, in pink brick and timber, richly gabled and chimneyed, where the Palmer family have lived since 1542. Also of endearing charm is Chenies Manor, near Amersham, in warm red brick, with its barley-sugar chimneystacks and stepped gables, its hidey-holes and secret passages.

▲ Polesden Lacey epitomises the elegant, restrained taste of the Regency period. Notable society parties were held here in Edwardian times

Tudor Country Life

Carried back in time to the Tudor period now, we should be alarmed by the lack of modern appliances and horrified by the painfulness of life, when babies were born and teeth pulled without 20th-century anaesthetics. We might also recoil from the blindingly garish colours that were liked at the time. Tudor people themselves, however, did not miss electric light, running hot water or television, which they had never known. On the contrary, they took pride in living in a time of unprecedented prosperity and comfort.

Houses were often H-shaped, with the great hall flanked by two wings, or E-shaped, with the great hall as the long stroke of the E. The entrance porch was the short arm, the family's private rooms were in the wing at one end and the kitchens and domestic quarters in the other. The house still swarmed with servants, children and dogs, and the great hall was used for entertaining, but there was more privacy for the family now, and many more rooms. The hearth moved from the centre of the great hall to one side, with a fireplace and a chimney to channel the smoke away, and many of the lesser rooms had their own fireplaces.

Windows now had glass in them, instead of horn. The walls were covered with wooden panelling or tapestries. The floors were still strewn with rushes or straw, but the very grandest houses were beginning to have oriental carpets. They would also have a long gallery, in which to take exercise when it was wet outdoors, and to hang pictures in as evidence of the family's wealth.

There was less furniture than we are accustomed to. Wooden beds, tables, cupboards, chests, stools and the occasional chair were heavy and clumsy. The nights were really dark, lit only by candles and rushlights. People generally got up when the sun did and went to bed soon after dark.

Georgian Grandeur

The Sackvilles were another rich court and London family. Sir Richard Sackville, who served in Henry VIII's treasury and married the daughter of a Lord Mayor of London, acquired so much money he was nicknamed 'Fillsack'. The money was inherited by his son, Sir Thomas, a minor poet and playwright who was an ornament of Queen Elizabeth's entourage. She gave him the Knole estate and early in the 17th century he imported 300 Italian workmen to enlarge and beautify it. The open well staircase was just coming in and Knole has a splendid example.

In the 18th century the house called The Moor at Rickmansworth in Hertfordshire, which had belonged to Cardinal Wolsey,

never meant for living in. They were for show and for entertaining, for dinners and masked balls, for guests to parade through in their smartest finery of silks and velvets, ruffles, wigs, powder and patches, while flirting, gossiping and intriguing.

The family had its own separate living quarters in rooms of more manageable proportions, and although there were still plenty of servants, they were kept out of the way in the basement, where the cooking and laundering were done, and in the attics where they slept. The household was still largely self-sufficient. Housewives and their domestics did their own dairying and butchering, brewing and baking, pickling and preserving, sewing and dressmaking. They doctored their families and made their own trusty herbal remedies. The mother of General James Wolfe, of Quebec House in Westerham, left posterity an alarming treatment for consumption, involving a peck of garden snails, washed in beer and roasted alive, mixed with a quart of sliced, salted earthworms beaten up with rosemary flowers and milk.

Family Cosiness
The 18th century saw the development of the villa as a more modest country residence in the fashionable Palladian manner. The main rooms were on the first floor, to give a better view of the countryside, with the servants beneath and the bedrooms above. A typical example is Asgill House, beside the Thames at Richmond, built for Sir Charles Asgill, a self-made London businessman. In the 1830s Decimus Burton laid out the Calverley Park housing estate in Tunbridge Wells, with smallish villas in an elegant Regency style, a row of shops and a private park. And soon rows and rows of Victorian terraced houses would be starting their long march out from the centre of London.

The Victorian era reacted against the simplicity, symmetry and pagan spirit of Georgian and Regency architecture. In a period of mounting affluence and self-confidence, Victorian architects and their clients felt free to pick and choose whatever style from the past appealed to them and to mingle elements from quite different styles. Cliveden was rebuilt as an Italian Renaissance palace by

Clandon Park is the work of Venetian architect Giacomo Leoni. He was employed by the wealthy Onslow family ▼

was bought by the financier Benjamin Hoskins Styles, rich on the proceeds of the South Sea Bubble. He hired Sir James Thornhill and Giacomo Leoni, a Venetian architect, to build him a Palladian mansion of classical grandeur. A hill which presumptuously obstructed his view of the Chess valley was swiftly removed, and the grounds were later landscaped by Capability Brown. The house is now a golf club and businessmen's foursomes drive and putt their way across the stately scene.

Leoni was also the architect of Clandon Park, outside Guildford, built for the Onslow family in the 1730s. A handsome, square house in red brick with stone dressings, it had formal gardens and canals which have not survived. Inside is a riot of Baroque plasterwork.

Visitors to the grandest 18th-century houses sometimes comment on how impossibly uncomfortable they must have been, but the state rooms were

▲ Knebworth was given its Gothic facelift with typical Victorian excess

Sir Charles Barry and there was a passion for medieval Gothic. At Knebworth House in Hertfordshire the Tudor manor house which the Lytton family had lived in since Columbus discovered the New World was transmogrified into an astonishing fantasy of towers, pinnacles, battlements, heraldic beasts and menacing gargoyles which looks as if it might have been designed by Edgar Allen Poe.

Although the Victorian upper class and middle class still relied heavily on servants, the demand for privacy grew stronger still and there was a shift away from the Georgian grand tradition of the house as a stage for showy entertaining, and over to family cosiness in rooms crowded to bursting with furniture, occasional tables, pianos, whatnots and stuffed birds under glass domes.

There was also a strong emphasis on health and cleanliness, with much improved drainage and running hot-water systems. Dining rooms were still kept well away from kitchens because Victorian households not only disliked cooking smells but regarded them as injurious to health. The coming of gaslight, oil lamps and finally electric light changed the rhythm of the day, which was no longer so closely bound to the sun. Households also grew far less self-sufficient as the industrial revolution and the railways introduced cheap, efficient and rapidly distributed domestic products.

Back to Old English

Next came a return to domestic architecture rooted in earlier English vernacular traditions. A pioneer was the architect George Devey who built 'Old English' cottages in timber and red brick at Penshurst in Kent in the 1850s. Another was Philip Webb, who designed The Red House at Bexleyheath in Kent for William Morris in 1859. In the 1870s Richard Norman Shaw built Grims Dyke (now a hotel), near Harrow Weald in Middlesex, later occupied by W S Gilbert, of the Gilbert and Sullivan partnership. A comfortable eight-bedroomed house in mellow red brick, it has half-timbered gables, deep-red tiles and tall chimneys, with a general effect of timeless peace and bees murmuring in the honeysuckle.

Sir Edwin Lutyens, the last English architect to enjoy really widespread confidence and esteem, started out in this English Vernacular manner. Munstead Wood, near Godalming in Surrey, which he built in 1896 for his friend Gertrude Jekyll, the great garden designer, is in his 'Surrey cottage' style, a long, low house with a huge, steeply plunging roof broken by massive gables, with tall chimneystacks. The Vernacular revival also influenced thousands of humbler houses in the suburbs.

Before World War I and the dramatic social changes of the 20th century, there was still time for country house creation on the grand scale. At Hever, in the early 1900s, the American millionaire William Waldorf Astor restored the crumbling castle of the Boleyns and created a thoroughly satisfying blend of Tudor and Edwardian interiors. With croquet on the lawn and cucumber sandwiches for tea, the Edwardian age moved through its golden afternoon towards sunset.

People and Places

The only Englishman ever to be elevated to the chair of St Peter was born in Hertfordshire, in the hamlet of Bedmond, near Kings Langley. Born in poverty, Nicholas Breakspear rose through the hierarchy of the Church to become pope as Adrian IV in 1154. There's a memorial to him in Abbots Langley church.

Abbots Langley is also the place where, in 1615, a 16-year-old girl named Elizabeth Jones married Thomas Greenhill. From then until she was 54 she never knew a year in which she was not pregnant. She bore her husband an astonishing total of 39 children.

The first Cox's orange pippin apples were grown by Richard Cox in the 1820s at Colnbrook, near Slough. The man who led the charge of the Light Brigade, the Earl of Cardigan, first saw the light of day in the Buckinghamshire village of Hambleden. William Penn, who founded the American state of Pennsylvania, came of Chilterns stock and is buried at Jordans. The melancholy poet William Cowper was born in the rectory at Berkhamsted and the empire-builder Cecil Rhodes in a Bishop's Stortford vicarage. Arthur Lasenby Liberty, son of a Chesham draper, founded the famous London department store and ended with a knighthood as squire of a Chilterns village, The Lee.

Other remarkable people and products of the area close to London include numerous kings and queens, three of the most admired books in the English language – *Paradise Lost*, *Pride and Prejudice* and *The Origin of Species* – 'Rule Britannia', the sculptures of Henry Moore, a profusion of poets and novelists prime ministers and pop stars, robbers, Robinson Crusoe and Frankenstein's monster.

Royal Memories

Almost every monarch of England since William the Conqueror has spent time at Windsor Castle, the royal family's principal home outside London. Edward III and Henry IV were both born in the castle and two kings of Scots, David II and James I, were held prisoner in it. Many monarchs lie buried in St George's Chapel, including Henry VIII and Charles I (complete with his head, which was sewn back on after his execution). Queen Victoria and her beloved Prince Albert lie interred in the beautiful royal mausoleum in the Home Park. The Duke and Duchess of Windsor are also buried in the

▲ George IV became Prince Regent in 1810 due to his father's derangement

royal cemetery, side by side.

The castle was enlarged and improved by successive generations. George III and his family were particularly fond of Windsor – though guests complained that the place was freezing cold – and spent so much time there that the royal standard, flown when the king was in residence, wore out and had to be replaced. The citizens of Windsor were fond of the royals in return and used to wander in and out of the castle and get in the royal family's way. It was partly to regain some privacy that George IV had the castle rebuilt in the mock medieval splendour of today.

Windsor Castle is also the home of the Order of the Garter, founded by Edward III. Great names of British history from the Black Prince to Sir Winston Churchill have attended services beneath a blaze of heraldry in St George's Chapel, and the knights gather there for a special ceremony every year in June.

It was at the Old Palace at Hatfield, in Hertfordshire, that the famous scene occurred in 1558, when a deputation of gentlemen rode posthaste from London to bring the 25-year-old Princess Elizabeth the news that her sister 'Bloody' Mary had died and she was now queen of England. They found her sitting beneath an oak tree, demurely reading an improving book and making a very attractive picture indeed. There is a fine portrait of her in the house today, and a pair of her silk stockings.

As a baby, the young Elizabeth did her teething at Hunsdon, east of Ware, in the care of her governess, Lady Byron. Her older brother and sister, Edward VI and Mary, had also been reared there, to get the benefit of the Hertfordshire air. Their alarming father, Henry VIII, liked the place and a country dance called 'Hunsdon House' is attributed to him. He kept his baby daughter desperately short of money. 'She hath neither gown nor kirtle nor petticoat', Lady Byron wrote pleadingly, 'nor no manner of linen nor foresmock nor kerchiefs . . .'.

Elizabeth's ill-fated mother, Anne Boleyn, was executed soon afterwards. She grew up at Hever Castle in Kent and Henry VIII went there courting her. Her sister Mary was Henry's mistress before Anne came in view. The imposing tomb of their father, Sir Thomas Boleyn, is in Hever church.

Foreign royalties, too, have left memories in England, from King Farouk of Egypt, who had a house in Old Windsor, to the Emperor Napoleon III of France, whose tomb is in the crypt of St Michael's, Farnborough, in Hampshire. With him are buried his wife, the ravishing Empress Eugenie, and their son, the Prince Imperial, who was killed in the Zulu War in Africa in 1879. The imperial family fled from France in 1870 and lived quietly in Chiselhurst in Kent.

Louis XVIII, exiled Bourbon king of France, lived at Hartwell House (now a hotel) near Aylesbury during the French Revolution. A group of French aristos sheltered from the fond embrace of Madame la Guillotine at Juniper Hall in Surrey, near Mickleham. They included the cynical diplomat Talleyrand and the writer Madame de Stäel.

Writers in Residence

It is a truth universally acknowledged that *Pride and Prejudice* is set in Hertfordshire. Jane Austen's fictitious town of Meryton is Hertford and the Bennet family's village might possibly be nearby Hertingfordbury.

Daniel Defoe wrote *Robinson Crusoe* in a cottage near Cranbrook in Kent. Frankenstein's monster was created in the blameless town of Marlow, by the Thames in Buckinghamshire, where the poet Shelley and his wife Mary lived in 1817. The poet worked on *The Revolt of Islam*, took long walks and went boating, while Mary was pregnant with both their daughter Clara and *Frankenstein*.

Kenneth Grahame lived further downstream, at Cookham Dean in Berkshire. He wrote *The Wind in the Willows* to amuse his young son, and it is on the

▲ Dickens, closely associated with Kent, died in 1870 at Gads Hill

stretch of the Thames between Marlow and Bourne End that the adventures of Rat and Mole, Toad and Badger should be imagined.

Sir Philip Sidney, poet and pattern of chivalry, grew up in the deep peace of the Kent countryside at Penshurst Place. John Milton finished *Paradise Lost* in 1665 in his 'pretty box' of a Buckinghamshire cottage in Chalfont St Giles, while the plague was finishing thousands of lives in London. Izaak Walton hymned the sweetness of Hertfordshire trout in *The Compleat Angler* and loved to fish the Lea. He found sweetness of another kind there too, for he married a girl from Little Berkhamsted.

Little Berkhamsted has other claims to fame. Beatrix Potter used to stay with her grandparents at Camfield Place, the house which Barbara Cartland, the romantic novelist, moved into in 1950. Brian Johnston, the cricket commentator, was born in Little

Elizabeth I was the unhappy progeny of Henry VIII and Anne Boleyn ▼

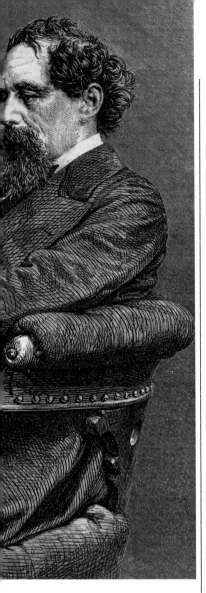

Berkhamsted, which for a time was home to the pop star Adam Ant.

A more formidable lion, Charles Dickens, is closely linked with Rochester and his last, unfinished, novel, *The Mystery of Edwin Drood*, is set in the city. His house outside the town on Gad's Hill is now a school. Dickens was a frequent visitor to Knebworth House in Hertfordshire, home of Edward Bulwer-Lytton, author of *The Last Days of Pompeii*, and took a lively part in the amateur theatricals there. One of the later Lyttons was Viceroy of India. His daughter, Lady Constance Lytton, was a leading suffragette and her sister, Emily, married the architect Edwin Lutyens.

Another Emily, Emily Sellwood, married a rising poet named Alfred Tennyson in the church at Shiplake by the Thames in Oxfordshire in 1850. Lewis Carroll used to stay with his aunts in Guildford and is buried in Guildford Cemetery. At Ayton St Lawrence in Hertfordshire lived George Bernard Shaw, from 1906. He was drawn there by a tombstone in the churchyard of a woman who lived to be 70, which said: 'Her time was short'. Shaw, encouraged, survived to 94.

Christina Rossetti lived for many years in the Buckinghamshire village of Holmer Green. Enid Blyton lived at Beaconsfield and so did G K Chesterton (his favourite pub was the White Hart). It was at Hatfield House, one January evening in 1912, that Harold Nicolson proposed to Vita Sackville-West and was accepted: she was one of the Sackvilles of Knole, outside Sevenoaks. They lived for some time at a house called The Long Barn in Sevenoaks Weald, where many Bloomsbury Group figures visited them. Virginia Woolf started to write *Orlando* there, with Vita as the central figure. The Nicolsons later lived at Sissinghurst Castle.

Buried in the quiet country churchyard at Penn in the Chilterns are Alison Uttley, author of *Little Grey Rabbit* and other much-loved children's books, and Elizabeth von Arnim, who wrote an earlier children's classic, *Elizabeth and Her German Garden*. The same quintessentially English graveyard also holds the ashes of Donald Maclean, of Burgess and Maclean fame, in an urn inscribed with a hammer and sickle.

Politicians

Many politicians have found the Home Counties convenient for a country house not too far from Westminster. Benjamin Disraeli was MP for Buckinghamshire from 1847 until he went to the Lords in 1880. He grew up at the manor house at Bradenham, his father's home, but is mainly associated with Hughenden, where he spent his happiest years and where he and his wife are both buried. Two other Victorian prime ministers, Lord Melbourne and Lord Palmerston, both lived at Brocket Hall, near Lemsford in Hertfordshire, as did Melbourne's wife, the notorious Lady Caroline Lamb, who was infatuated with Lord Byron. The great Duke of Wellington, who was never infatuated, lived calmly at Strafield Saye in Hampshire.

John Hampden, a key figure in the resistance to Charles I, lived at Great Hampden in the Chilterns (the house is now a school) and is buried in the churchyard. Close by, and closely guarded, is Chequers, which every prime minister since Lloyd George has used as a country retreat.

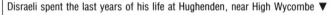

Disraeli spent the last years of his life at Hughenden, near High Wycombe ▼

▲ Sir Winston Churchill, statesman

Near Westerham in Kent, Chartwell is a museum to Sir Winston Churchill. The house was his country home for 40 years. Eileen Joyce, the concert pianist, had a cottage near by in the 1960s and her Alsatian attacked Rufus, the Churchills' poodle, but the owners remained friendly.

Sir Winston's ancestor, John Churchill, Duke of Marlborough, married a beautiful spitfire of a Hertfordshire girl, Sarah Jennings, born at Sandridge. They lived in St Albans, in Holywell House, and both Queen Anne and George I visited them there.

A formidable figure of a later day was Lady Astor, who lived at Cliveden with its sumptuous gardens beside the river near Maidenhead. Thomas Arne wrote 'Rule Britannia' for a masque there, when the house was owned by the Prince of Wales, George III's father. Prince Frederick, known to everybody as 'poor Fred', loved cricket, which killed him, for he died at Cliveden in 1751 after being hit in the chest by a cricket ball. The Astors and their friends in the 1930s, 'the Cliveden set', favoured appeasing Hitler. The place is best-known, however, for an incident in 1961 when Christine Keeler met John Profumo there, which led to a scandal that set all Britain by the ears.

Old Boys

The country churchyard of Gray's famous 'Elegy' is at Stoke Poges and the poet is buried in it. He also wrote an ode on 'a Distant Prospect of Eton College', of which he was an old boy. Eton has educated more cabinet ministers and other establishment figures than any rival: among them the two Pitts, Charles James Fox, the Duke of Wellington, Mr Gladstone and Harold Macmillan, as well as Shelley, Swinburne and George Orwell. Old Etonians also include Ian Fleming, the creator of James Bond, the heroic Polar explorer Captain Oates and the jazz trumpeter Humphrey Lytelton.

Among other schools in the area, Charterhouse, near Godalming in Surrey, taught John Wesley, Thackeray, Baden Powell and Vaughan Williams. Clement Attlee went to Haileybury in Hertfordshire. Tonbridge educated E M Forster and many a fine cricketer, Colin Cowdrey among them. Numerous distinguished army officers, including Field Marshal Montgomery, have emerged from the Royal Military Academy at Sandhurst. Berkhamsted School taught Graham Greene and his brother Hugh (Director General of the BBC). Their father was the headmaster. Graham Greene used to play Russian roulette with a loaded revolver on Berkhamsted Common.

Musical and Artistic Talent

Samuel Palmer, the visionary landscape artist, lived at Shoreham in the Darent valley of Kent, and painted the surrounding country in the most formative period of his life. The studio of G F Watts, 'the English Michelangelo', can be enjoyed at Compton in Surrey. Sir Stanley Spencer lived almost his whole life at Cookham in Berkshire, where

Stanley Spencer RA spent much of his life at Cookham ▼

▲ Highwayman Claude Duval charmed and alarmed the ladies by turns

the Thames and local scenes and people inspired much of his work. Henry Moore lived and worked at 'Hoglands' in the Hertfordshire village of Perry Green near Much Hadham, and many of his most famous works were produced there.

On the musical front, Frederick Delius lies buried in the churchyard at Limpsfield in Surrey. Selections from his music were conducted by Sir Thomas Beecham at the funeral, and a blackbird sang sweetly in the yew trees. Beecham himself, incidentally, was buried in the huge Brookwood Cemetery near Woking, as were Rebecca West and the thriller writer Dennis Wheatley. Recently, however, Sir Thomas was moved and now he too lies in Limpsfield.

Charles Darwin wrote *The Origin of Species* in his study at Down House in Kent. His niece Caroline married Josiah Wedgwood of the pottery dynasty and they lived at Leith Hill Place, just below the famous Surrey beauty spot, where they planted the rhododendrons and azaleas which make such a show today. Their three small daughters used to assist scientific Uncle Charles with his observations of earthworms. One of them, Margaret, was the mother of

Ralph Vaughan Williams, who was brought up at Leith Hill Place and later lived in Dorking.

Further west in Surrey, Haslemere is known for its connections with the Dolmetsch family. Arnold Dolmetsch settled there in 1917. A player and restorer of early musical instruments, he set up workshops and started the Haslemere Festival. He was a major figure in the revival of interest in early music and the renewed popularity of the recorder.

The Edge of Society

A gravestone in the churchyard of Northchurch in Hertfordshire marks the last resting place of Peter the Wild Boy, who was found in Germany in the 1720s and brought to England. He moved on all fours, ate grass and could not speak, and it was thought he might have been nurtured by wolves. Attempts to teach him to speak failed and he spent the rest of his life in Northchurch, kindly treated, wearing a collar round his neck with his address on it for when he wandered off.

Hertfordshire was notorious for its witches, and the last witch trial in England was held at Hertford in 1712, when Jane

Wenham was condemned to hang. She was afterwards reprieved and pardoned. It took a long time for fear of witchcraft to die, and in 1751 villagers at Wilstone, near Tring, 'swam' an elderly couple as suspected witches and killed them both.

One of the highwaymen who preyed on travellers on Bagshot Heath and Hounslow Heath was the gallant Frenchman, Claude Duval, as notorious for his way with the ladies as for his daring robberies. He was caught in London in 1670 and hanged, still only in his twenties. The highwayman tradition was brought up to date in 1962, when the Great Train Robbery, carried out on the main railway line north of Cheddington in Buckinghamshire, netted £2.5 million in used notes.

The Rye House plot, to assassinate Charles II and his brother, the future James II, on their way back to London from Newmarket, was hatched in 1683 at the Rye House, near Hoddesden in Hertfordshire. The most notorious figure in the area's past, however, is probably Sir Francis Dashwood of West Wycombe Park, founder of the blasphemous Hell Fire Club (see page 71).

Pubs and Inns

Standing beside its village green in the pleasant Weald of Surrey is one of the great old inns of England. Grandly half-timbered and massively beamed, wreathed by lilac and laburnum as the summer comes in, the Crown at Chiddingford has stood there for 700 years. More than 20 generations of locals and passers-by, from ploughmen to royalty, have found a welcome and slaked a thirst there since the inn was built in 1285 as an overnight stop for pilgrims on their way between Winchester and Canterbury.

By 1383 the inn had been leased to a landlord named Godfayre, who, despite his encouragingly pious name, was in trouble more than once for over-charging and giving short measure. In 1552 the young King Edward VI put up at the Crown, though as he brought a retinue of 4,000 people with him, most of his party had to camp outside. Across the border into Kent, at Speldhurst, is another veteran of the same breed, the George and Dragon, with a history as long or longer.

The area around London has a wealth of old hostelries, which over the centuries have become an integral part of the landscape. Many of them lie along the busy main routes into and out of London – or what were once the main routes – but others nestle in quiet villages that were always off the beaten track.

Before the Flood

The ancient and octagonal Old Fighting Cocks in St Albans, whose garden runs down to the River Ver, engagingly claims to date from 'before the Flood', but this is not a reference to Noah's Ark, but to a more modest overflow of the Ver at the beginning of the 16th century.

This fiercely-named inn was originally a peaceable dovecote, which stood elsewhere and was moved to this site in the 1400s. It was being used as an inn by 1599 and Oliver Cromwell stayed a night or two in 1648. In Stuart and Georgian times it was a cockfighting centre and part of today's saloon bar was the brick cockpit, down steps on which the spectators sat and shouted their favourites on.

Another historic pub patronised by Oliver Cromwell is the King's Head at Aylesbury, tucked away among alleys off the market square. It may have been the guesthouse of the local friary originally, but was later a coaching inn, and later still a temperance hotel until rescued from this dolorous condition by the National Trust.

The Crown has been the centre of village life at Chiddingfold for centuries ▼

Coaching Days

In Tudor times, in an age of peace and prosperity, people travelled more and new inns opened to meet the demand. Scenes for many a Tudor-period film have been shot in the National Trust's village of Chiddingstone in Kent, where the 16th-century Castle Inn stands in its soothing warmth of red-brick and tile-hung walls opposite the leaning tombstones in the churchyard.

The great coaching inns saw their heyday in the 18th century, with their ample Georgian frontages, their capacious yards and stables. There the horses were changed, while the traveller could have something to eat and get warm by a roaring fire. Many new inns were built and existing ones modernised and enlarged. The George at Odiham in Hampshire, for instance, and the White Horse in Dorking both conceal Tudor rooms behind their smooth Georgian faces.

At West Wycombe on the London-to-Oxford road, the landlord of the George and Dragon kept carrier pigeons to convey messages for passengers stranded in bad weather. Today the pub is haunted by a ghost which plays the fiddle. There's another at the White Hart in Chalfont St Peter: a 19th-century landlord named Donald Ross so enjoyed serenading his guests that he has never been able to stop.

A famous inn on the London-to-Brighton road was the

▲ The King's Head at Aylesbury, one of the town's most historic buildings

George at Crawley, where the Prince Regent changed his horses on his way to the Pavilion and the sea-breezes (and the inn appears in Conan Doyle's *Rodney Stone*). The London coaches were stopping there hourly in the 1830s, but the stagecoaches were soon to be driven out of business by the railways and the coaching inns were eclipsed until the coming of the motor car restored them to vigorous life.

What's in a Name

Inn names are a rich source of interest. Many of them are drawn from the animal kingdom and country pursuits: the Bull, the Greyhound, the Plough, the Bat and Ball, the Bird in Hand.

Many pub names are a mystery ▼

Long-distance coaching reached a peak in the 1820s and inns were built along the major routes to meet the needs of travellers and coachmen ▼

Some preserve the names and coats of arms of local landowning families. The pub at Penshurst in Kent is the Leicester Arms because the Sidneys of Penshurst Place were at one time Earls of Leicester. The Rosebery Arms at Cheddington, Buckinghamshire, is near Mentmore, formerly the stately home of the Earls of Rosebery. The Sackvilles of Knole became Dukes of Dorset,

▲ The White Horse in Dorking's High Street is one of the oldest of the town's inns. It was formerly an important coaching stop

hence the Dorset Arms pubs in Sevenoaks and Withyham, and also the former Three Cats in Sevenoaks, named after the three leopards of the Sackvilles' heraldry.

Some pub names honour other local notables. The Dimsdale Arms in Hertford was named after an 18th-century doctor who daringly inoculated Catherine the Great of Russia against smallpox. The Crown and Cushion at Minley in Hampshire is named after local hero Colonel Blood, who stole the crown jewels in 1671 and nearly got away with it. The Pineapple in Dorney is a reminder that the first pineapples in England were grown at Dorney Court. The Marlow Donkey is named affectionately after a little steam train that used to puff its way between Marlow and Bourne End: it can be seen on the sign.

Other names are unusual, strange or unfathomable – the products of imagination, whimsy or jokiness: the Hit or Miss at Amersham in Buckinghamshire; the Jekyll and Hyde at Stratfield Turgis, Hampshire; the Thirst and Last at Hildenborough, Kent; the Railway and Bicycle in Sevenoaks; the Frog and Bucket at Ide Hill, Kent, and the Slug and Lettuce at Winkfield, Berkshire. The Viper at Mill Green in Essex is thought to be the only pub of that name in the country which must surely also be true of the Bel and the Dragon at Cookham in Berkshire and The Rorty Crankle at Plaxtol in Kent.

Claims to Fame

Some inns cherish connections with famous people and famous books. William Cobbett of *Rural Rides* fame was born in the Farnham pub which now bears his name, when it was the Jolly Farmer. The body of Lord Byron rested for a night at the White Hart in Welwyn on its way north for burial in 1824. Tsar Peter the Great put up at the King's Arms in Godalming on his way to London in the 1690s.

Charles Dickens is fondly remembered with a collection of memorabilia in the old Leather Bottle at Cobham in Kent, which features in the *Pickwick Papers*. So does the Bull in Rochester, now the Royal Victoria and Bull, which also appears in *Great Expectations*. An Essex pub, the King's Head at Chigwell, was the model for the 'Maypole' in *Barnaby Rudge*. Rupert Brooke used to drink beer and write poetry in the Chilterns at the Pink and Lily at Speen, while the George at Chertsey is mentioned in *The War of the Worlds* by H G Wells.

Izaak Walton probably lifted a glass or two in the Fish and Eels, on the Essex bank of the Lea near Dobbs Weir. The Compleat Angler by the Thames in Marlow is named in his honour: it was previously the Angler's Rest. Waterside pubs have their own special flavour, like the delightful Thames Court at Shepperton Lock with its 1930s atmosphere. The Greyhound at Chalfont St Peter is built partly across the River Mimram.

Other hostelries make other claims on the attention. The Plough in the Surrey hamlet of Coldharbour is the highest pub in south-east England at 800ft above sea level. The Little Gem at Aylesford claims to be the smallest pub in Kent, and so does the Two Brewers in Rochester, which is tiny enough to be One Brewer. And at Horndon on the Hill in Essex a collection of moth-eaten hot-cross-buns dangles from the ceiling of the Bell. One has been added every year this century, in a touch of eccentricity that completes the picture of the amiable English pub.

The Capital City

London has something for everyone and an experience for every mood. Whether you want to see the Changing of the Guard or admire the glittering cavalry in the Mall; brood among the memorials in Poets' Corner in Westminster Abbey; gaze at Egyptian mummies and Assyrian winged bulls in the British Museum; shout for your side at the Cup Final; gasp at the horrors in Madame Tussaud's; enjoy the spring crocuses in the parks; see the barges and police launches butting through the choppy Thames; take in a theatre or take afternoon tea at the Ritz or price a grand piano at Harrods; or simply sit and watch half the world go by – London will meet the need.

London is Britain's largest and richest city, the place where the country is run and decisions are made. It is also the cultural capital. It has the best theatre, the first-run cinemas, two opera houses, symphony orchestras, ballet companies. It has the priciest and most avant-garde art galleries, the most exclusive and expensive shops. It stages most of the major shows, exhibitions and sporting events. This remarkable wealth and variety of attractions makes it a richly rewarding city to explore.

London's People

London has always been a magnet to people of talent and

Blue plaques show where persons of note used to live ▼

ambition. As the top of the ladder, it has drawn to itself men and women determined to get on in the world. From Pitt to Churchill, from Shakespeare to Dr Johnson to Charles Dickens, from Garrick to Olivier, the city has been the arena for the greatest figures in Britain's history. One of the pleasures of walking in London is to spot the blue plaques on houses where famous people lived and the statues in squares and gardens: from Charlie Chaplin in Leicester Square to the great Duke of Wellington on his Waterloo charger, Copenhagen, at Hyde Park Corner.

From its beginnings as an outpost of warm Mediterranean civilisation in the cold, barbarous lands of the north, London has recruited its population as much or more by immigration as by natural increase. French Protestants fleeing from persecution came to London in the 17th century, and many of them settled in Soho, which has been foreign territory ever since. In the years of famine in the 1840s Irish immigration rose dramatically. Later in the 19th century Jews fleeing pogroms in Russia and Eastern Europe crowded into Whitechapel. Chinese settled in Limehouse, close to the docks, inspiring thrillers about opium dens and sinister slant-eyed master criminals. After World War II numerous immigrants arrived from the West Indies, Pakistan and Bangladesh.

The result is London's rich mixture of traditions, customs and cuisines. You can buy West Indian delicacies in the street markets in Brixton and Shepherd's Bush, there are mosques in Regent's Park and Whitechapel, Arab butchers in Bayswater and London has some of the best Indian and Chinese restaurants in the world.

Getting Around

The best way to see London and experience its atmosphere is undoubtedly to walk. When the legs get weary, a seat on one of the red double-decker buses provides a grandstand view of the streets, buildings and people for a very reasonable fee. The tube will usually move you faster, or there are taxis, or you can hire a bicycle if you like.

Another enjoyable way to see the city is by boat on the river. The Thames was the primary geographical reason for London's founding and existence, because it provided an easy route to Europe, and later to the wider world.

The river divides London into northern and southern halves. The northern half, which is much the more important, divides roughly into three sections: the West End, the City and the East End. The West End is smart, fashionable London. The City, with a capital C, is the financial centre and the place where London began. Over on the southern side of the Thames at this point is the South Bank cultural area, with the Royal Festival Hall and the National Theatre, which developed after the Festival of Britain in 1951.

Further on downstream, the East End, the old working-class London of cockneys and rhyming slang, has been substantially rebuilt. The run-down docks of the Isle of Dogs have blossomed as Docklands, an expensive office and residential area in the latest architectural fashions.

The Beginnings

London's history stretches back almost 2,000 years, to the Roman invasion of Britain in AD43. The Romans established a supply depot at the highest point on the Thames to which

L.C.C.

CHARLES DICKENS
1812-1870
Novelist
Lived Here

their ships could navigate up river. They built quays and a bridge, close to where London Bridge is now, and the new settlement became the capital of Roman Britain and a thriving commercial town. A defensive wall was built round it, two miles long, parts of which are still standing – the oldest major historic monument in the city.

After the Romans withdrew from Britain, the invading Saxons (the English) founded a town of their own to the west of the Roman one. It has left its memory behind as Aldwych ('old town'), but it proved vulnerable to Vikings raiding up the Thames in their dragon-prowed longships. In the 9th century King Alfred moved the town back inside the Roman wall.

Church and State

Over to the west, one-and-a-half miles away along the Thames, Benedictine monks had built a small monastery on Thorney Island in a dreary wasteland of marshes and brambles: 'a terrible place', someone in the 8th century called it. The saintly King Edward the Confessor gave the monks a new abbey church in the 11th century, and to keep a close eye on the work built a palace there and moved into it.

The result was the creation of two Londons, in effect: the commercial centre of the City and the royal and political centre at 'the west minster', as the new church was called. Rebuilt in spectacular grandeur in the Middle Ages, the church became Westminster Abbey, crowded with the monuments of the illustrious dead, where every crowned monarch since William the Conqueror has been formally enthroned.

The royal palace, after many vicissitudes and rebuildings, has become the Houses of Parliament, rising in Victorian mock-Tudor magnificence beside the Thames, where MPs take their teas and their ease on the terrace on sunny afternoons. At the northern end of the building is one of London's best-loved landmarks – the tall clock-tower which houses Big Ben, the cracked 13-ton bell whose deep tones sound the hours over the traffic hurrying across Westminster Bridge. Each of the minute hands on the four huge clock faces is as long as a double-decker bus is high.

Close by stand the government offices along Whitehall. In Downing Street is the modest 18th-century house which is the prime minister's London residence. The Cabinet War Rooms hidden in a deep bunker, where Winston Churchill ran the war effort during the Blitz, are open to all-comers now. Wreaths of red poppies rest at the foot of the Cenotaph, a simple memorial to those who fell in the two World Wars. Outside the Horse Guards building the motionless cavalry sentries sit astride their horses while the tourist cameras click.

Looking towards Blackfriars Bridge ▼

▲ The Tower of London, one of the city's greatest tourist attractions

Traitor's Gate

The two Londons – the City and Westminster – joined up as courtiers, noblemen and officials built themselves town houses along the river between. Meantime in the City, William the Conqueror had built the formidable fortress which has commanded the Thames ever since. The Tower of London has a grim place in London's story, with its ominous ravens, its moats and its battlements. It was a prison for political offenders and suspects, who were brought by water to the dark portico of Traitor's Gate. Many a well-born head fell to the axe on Tower Green, or on Tower Hill outside the walls. The bodies were buried in the Tower's chapel of St Peter, which has an uneasy reputation today as a place you might prefer not to spend the night in. The heads were parboiled, daubed with tar as a preservative and stuck up on spikes above the southern gateway of London Bridge. London's past horrors are today recreated with grisly realism at the London Dungeon, in the vaults under London Bridge Station on the south side of the river. The screams you hear there may be your own.

The last state prisoner in the Tower was Rudolf Hess, incarcerated there after his mysterious arrival in Scotland in 1941. Instead of prisoners the fortress today guards the crown jewels. Among them is St Edward's Crown, used at every coronation since Charles II's, while the fabulous Koh-i-noor diamond from India, 'the mountain of light', gleams in the crown of Queen Elizabeth the Queen Mother. This crown was made by Garrard's, the royal jewellers, who have a shop in Regent Street.

In 1666 a fire in a baker's shop in Pudding Lane, fanned by an unforgiving breeze, went completely out of control and burned down four-fifths of the City in four days. Londoners were as tough and resilient then as they were to show themselves in the Blitz three centuries later. The City was swiftly rebuilt, while Sir Christopher Wren's immense Baroque church of St Paul raised its massive dome in majesty to the sky. Wren also designed the beautiful parish churches which today are dwarfed by the City's hulking office buildings.

City Lights

The City is all business and money. The West End, with its theatres, restaurants, night spots and glamorous shops, is where Londoners go for a night out or something special to buy. The hub of it is Piccadilly Circus, where the giant advertising signs flash and glimmer, while a grinding entanglement of traffic fights its way past the statue of *Eros*, with his butterfly wings, aiming his delicate bow in the general direction of Lillywhite's, the famous sports outfitters.

The Soho area to the north is London's principal restaurant and sex-show district, with an atmosphere curiously compounded of *haute cuisine* and sleaze. London's Chinatown is here, and there is a lively open-air market in Berwick Street.

To the south, the pigeons coo and flutter in Trafalgar Square, where the 17ft statue of

Britain's most famous store – Harrods ▼

Britain's greatest naval hero gazes impassively from the top of the 170ft Nelson's Column: on which 14 people sat down to a precarious rump steak dinner before the statue was hoisted up into place in 1842. The National Gallery commands the north side of the square, with the country's finest collection of Old Master paintings (modern art is in the Tate Gallery on Millbank).

In the Covent Garden area the famous fruit and vegetable market has departed and the handsome old market building with its surrounding piazza has become a lively forum of restaurants, boutiques, buskers and street entertainment. In the Royal Opera House legendary singers from Caruso to Callas and Patti to Pavarotti have kept audiences in the opulent auditorium enthralled.

Shopping is one of the great pleasures of the West End. Harrods in its terracotta palace on the Brompton Road is the most famous shop on earth. It will sell you anything from a pot of caviar to a parrot while you are alive and bury you with dignified discretion when you are dead. Fortnum and Mason on Piccadilly is famous for traditional British delicacies and there's a line of department stores moored like battleships along Oxford Street. More enticing, perhaps, is London's extraordinary range of specialist

shops. You can buy perfumes at Floris, chocolates at Charbonnel et Walker, suits at Gieves and Hawkes, beads at Ells and Farrier, model soldiers at Tradition, lingerie at Janet Reger, a swordstick at James Smith and Sons.

Over to the west lie the areas where London expanded in the 18th and early 19th centuries, spreading over the open country of Mayfair and Belgravia, and swallowing up the rural villages of Knightsbridge, Kensington and Chelsea. Designed for the well-to-do, the new estates were laid out in elegant, regular terraces, squares and crescents, with mews and service areas at the back. Many of the houses have been converted into flats and offices, but these are still among the pleasantest parts of London to stroll in.

Green and Royal London

Though heavily populated and crammed almost to suffocation with people, traffic and noise, London has a surprising amount of open space and greenery. The oldest of the city's parks is St James's Park, known for its wildfowl and its charming lake. In Hyde Park and Kensington Gardens people go boating on the Serpentine or riding in Rotten Row, sailing toy boats on the Round Pond or listening to soapbox oratory at Speakers' Corner.

The principal parks are royal property and were originally hunting grounds where Henry VIII and his courtiers pursued the deer or pleasure gardens where Charles II strolled with his mistresses and his spaniels. Much of London's rich heritage of pageantry is royal, too: from Trooping the Colour in June, when the Guards and Household Cavalry parade in a blazing panoply of massed bands, marching men and jingling horses, to the State Opening of Parliament in the autumn, when the Queen rides to Westminster in the Irish State Coach.

Tourists cluster to watch the Changing of the Guard at Buckingham Palace, the royal family's principal London home since Queen Victoria's time. In the Edwardian era it was made the focal point of a regal ceremonial arena, expressing the grandeur of the British Empire. The Empire has gone, but the grandeur remains.

Gazetteer

▲ Hampton Court

Each entry in the Gazetteer has the atlas page number on which the place can be found and its National Grid reference included under the heading. An explanation of how to use the National Grid is given on page 82.

▲ Abinger Hammer's clock-tower stands on the site of an old forge

ABINGER HAMMER
MAP REF: 91TQ0947

The river here powered ironworking mills during the Middle Ages and the village takes its name from the hammers that were used. The hammer ponds, which provided the water to power the mills, are now used as watercress beds. Projecting across the A25 is the famous and much-photographed hammer-clock. The bell is struck on the hour by a figure representing 'Jack the Smith'.

Near by is **Gomshall**, on the Tillingbourne, and Gomshall Mill is now a crafts showroom, also serving teas.

ALBURY
MAP REF: 91TQ0447

A string of pleasing villages lie on or just south of the A25 east of Guildford, linked by the tiny, but historically important, River Tillingbourne. Moving from west to east, the visitor starts with Albury, whose gardens dip their feet in the river. Albury could be a template for anyone wishing to study the development of an estate village. Originally grouped round the mansion of Albury Park, it was demolished and rebuilt during the 19th century. Much of the village is Gothic in style, with a preponderance of chimneys – a reflection of the house, which contains more chimneys than

Mock-Tudor chimneys of all kinds are a distinctive feature of Albury ▶

rooms! Albury Park is not open to the public, but the delightful gardens are well worth visiting, as is the original church in the park. Deserted since 1842, it is maintained by the Redundant Churches Fund.

North of the A25, between Albury and Shere, lies the **Silent Pool**, with wonderfully clear waters filtered through the chalk downs rising above. Naturally, there is a sad, but apocryphal, story attached to it, in this case that of a maiden disturbed by King John while bathing naked in the pool. Frightened, she retreated, lost her footing and was drowned.

ALDBURY
MAP REF: 86SP9612

If visitors experience a sense of *déjà vu* in Aldbury, it is probably because they recall innumerable British films made in the forties and fifties and now shown on television, demonstrating that the village was regularly used for outdoor settings. If Shere can claim to be Surrey's prettiest village, then this may well be Hertfordshire's. A large village green, complete with stocks and pond, is surrounded by old brick cottages, several with exposed timber frames. Stocks Road, with its rather self-consciously handsome houses, leads to Stocks, once the home of Mrs Humphry Ward, a Victorian novelist perhaps best remembered today through the memoirs of her nephew, the scientist Aldous Huxley, and through her son-in-law, the historian, G M Trevelyan.

The wooded slopes of the Chiltern escarpment give the final touch to the village, rising like a protective curtain behind it.

AMERSHAM
MAP REF: 86SU9597

Before and after World War II, thousands of people wishing to escape from London at weekends travelled to Amersham by tube or Green Line. From here they could explore the Chiltern Hills. Today the motor car has extended their range, and the M25 and M40 have become the preferred routes for those aiming for the countryside north-west of the capital.

Inns are often indicative of the age and importance of a town, and Amersham boasts several, including the Crown Hotel with its 16th-century interior, and the Swan Inn, where the last major rebuilding was in 1643. Typical of several houses in the town is the

▲ The attractive Old Town of Amersham in the Misbourne valley

timber-framed King's Arms, while the 17th-century redbrick market hall demonstrates changing fashions in building materials. The hall was built by a descendant of Sir Francis Drake, and several other reminders exist of the family's long connection with Amersham, including the Drake almshouses. The Church of St Mary has many monuments to the family, and Shardeloes, their mansion, now converted into flats but with a garden by Repton, can be seen from the A413 at the northern end of the town.

At **Amersham-on-the-Hill**, the Martyr's Memorial is reached from the churchyard and commemorates seven Lollards burned at the stake in the 16th century. There is a story that the daughter of one was forced to light the fire in which her father died.

ASCOTT HOUSE
MAP REF: 86SP8923

Originally a small, timbered Jacobean farmhouse, built for the local Dormer family, Ascott was considerably expanded in the 19th and 20th centuries when it became one of several properties in the area owned by members of the Rothschild family. It now resembles an overgrown, but pleasing, Tudor cottage. The garden, with its rare specimen trees and attractive bulb- and border-planting, was laid out in the 19th century. The centrepiece of the terrace garden is a very large topiary sundial with the inscription 'light and shade by turn but love always' picked out in golden yew. The house's main feature is Anthony de Rothschild's collection, mainly works of 17th-century Dutch and 18th- and 19th-century English painters, with superb examples of Chinese Ming porcelain (see page 78).

One mile away is the village of **Wing**, with its fine 10th-century Church of All Saints'. Its Saxon chancel arch is the largest surviving example in the country and another unusual distinction is that one of its priests was hanged at Tyburn – not for his faith, but for forgery! The almshouses, with dormer windows, were built by the Dormer family in 1569.

ASHRIDGE
MAP REF: 86SP9912

A house has existed on this site for many centuries, but the present building, set in glorious parkland, is almost entirely the work of the Wyatt family. An earlier, monastic building, the 'College of Bonhommes', passed to the Crown at the Dissolution and was acquired by Thomas Egerton in 1604. The estate remained in the hands of his descendants, the Bridgewaters and Brownlows, until the death of the 3rd Earl Brownlow in 1921. The possibility that the estate might be sold piecemeal resulted in a vigorous campaign, led by the Prime Minister, Stanley Baldwin, to raise money to purchase some 1,700 acres on behalf of the National Trust.

The house was sold separately, becoming Ashridge College and establishing an international reputation for its management courses. Its interior is now enjoyed mainly by students but it is sometimes open to the public – usually at summer weekends. The rich 19th-century decorations remain, and in particular, the library and main conference room, with its fine painted ceiling, cannot fail to delight visitors, while the lovely chapel is widely accepted as the best surviving example of James Wyatt's medieval style. The pleasure garden is by Repton, his last major commission and one of his favourites.

In recent years the National Trust has extended its Ashridge holdings to 4,000 acres of farm, wood, down and commonland along the Chiltern escarpment. The focal point is the granite Bridgewater Monument, a memorial to the 3rd Duke of Bridgewater, a notable pioneer of the canal system. Many splendid walks have been created through the woods and commons, and because the estate possesses two distinct types of soil there is an opportunity to study a wide range of wildlife. Easily handled, electrically-powered vehicles allow visitors with disabilities to explore two walks around the monument.

ASTON ROWANT
MAP REF: 86SU7299

This National Nature Reserve lies across the M40 at the dramatic point where it slashes through a deep cutting before beginning its rapid descent to the wide Oxfordshire plain. Containing some 300 acres of chalk grassland, scrub with ash, hawthorn and an important area of juniper together with beechwood, the reserve aims to conserve both the varied habitats and the numbers of specialised species associated with them. Particularly important are the downland plants, encouraged by close-cropping by sheep, and the butterfly population.

From the summit of Beacon Hill the view is, if anything, more striking than from the road, with the Cotswolds on the far horizon. The reserve possesses a fine interpretative centre with displays on the wildlife of the reserve, and a waymarked trail, carefully planned to include all types of habitat. The village of Aston Rowant has some charming flint and brick cottages around a green.

AYLESBURY

MAP REF: 86SP8213

The county town since the 16th century, Aylesbury suffered unsympathetic redevelopment in the 1960s when some of the atmosphere of the old town was lost, but nevertheless much remains for visitors' enjoyment. The county hall in the market square is mostly 18th-century, although the courtroom, used for the trial of the Great Train Robbers, has been restored following a fire in 1970.

There is a bronze statue to the politician John Hampden in the square, while across it, down a narrow alley, is the King's Head, a coaching inn owned by the National Trust. This lovely old building dates back to the 15th century and some contemporary stained glass survives in a window in the lounge bar. There are two 15th-century houses in Church Street, opposite the museum which has several permanent displays, including a gallery of Buckinghamshire rural life. Another noteworthy building is Prebendal House, John Wilkes' home when he was MP for Aylesbury.

▲ Shaw did much of his writing in the garden shed at Shaw's Corner

through the charming garden to the revolving wooden shed in which he did much of his writing. The sheer ordinariness of the house and its furnishings heightens the sense of a 'real' home, a place where visitors feel able to relax.

The villages contain some very good houses, several half-timbered, including, at Ayot St Lawrence, the Brocket Arms, a true village inn. If the houses are entirely in character, it would be difficult to imagine two more unlikely churches in adjoining villages than those of Ayot St Lawrence and Ayot St Peter. Ayot St Lawrence has two; the old church, about 1300, is

Barges moored in the canal basin at Aylesbury – the terminus of a branch of the Grand Union – make an attractive scene ▼

THE AYOTS

MAP REF: 87TL1916

The quiet villages comprising the Ayots – Ayot Green, St Peter and St Lawrence – lie close to the A1(M), yet would probably be largely neglected were it not for Shaw's Corner, the house where George Bernard Shaw lived from 1906 until his death in 1950. The National Trust, with a certain degree of artifice, maintains this undistinguished villa as if Shaw had simply slipped outside, perhaps

ruined and locked. Its destruction was carried out by Sir Lionel Lyde, an 18th-century owner of Ayot House, who replaced it with a church set in fields on the edge of the village. The small new church stands behind a grand Greek portico with colonnades leading to open pavilions. As an eyecatcher, delightful; as a village church, dottily incongruous – but then Sir Lionel and his wife are buried in separate transepts, he seeing no reason why, having been joined in this life, they should continue the

arrangement in the next! After this, the Arts and Crafts Church of St Peter, of varicoloured patterned brick, appears *almost* appropriate for its setting, while poor Ayot Green can only offer a rather unusual part-timbered tollhouse of *c.*1730.

BEACONSFIELD

MAP REF: 86SU9490

Developed as a staging point at the crossing of two important roads – from London to Oxford and Windsor to Aylesbury – much of the old town of Beaconsfield has survived, retaining many attractive 17th-century houses. Three coaching inns are still in business, although the method of transport has altered, as has their appearance. Beaconsfield has grown considerably during this century but, happily, the new town section is separate from the old.

Writers and politicians seem to find Beaconsfield and its environs attractive – the poet Edmund Waller was an early resident and, in this century, another poet, the American Robert Frost lived here as did G K Chesterton and the prolific children's writer, Enid Blyton. Edmund Burke was born, lived and died here. He and Waller are both buried in the churchyard of St Mary and All Saints'.

On the edge of the new town is **Bekonscot Model Village**, the oldest in the world (it celebrated its Diamond Jubilee in 1989). Planned on a scale of 1 inch to 1 foot, it contains over 70 cottages, farms and countryside. A railway with many engines and five stations is another feature. The present Queen, when a child, was a regular visitor.

BELTRING

MAP REF: 93TQ6747

Hops and Kent have been associated since the 15th century and Whitbread now have a fascinating agricultural museum at their Hop Farm. The farm contains the largest group of Victorian oast-houses and galleried barns in the world – 25 oasts with gleaming white-painted cowls, set among traditional Kent hop-fields.

The museum concentrates on demonstrating traditional methods of hop growing and drying, and explains the rural crafts associated with beer production. Early hop-farming implements are on show, with blacksmiths' and wheelwrights' tools and dairy equipment. Among other farm animals the magnificent shire horses – some retired from pulling the famous London drays, some enjoying an annual rest – attract most attention but, with a nature trail, craft centre and fishing ponds, all visitors will find something of interest.

BERKHAMSTED
MAP REF: 86SP9907

There has probably been a settlement here since the Romans built Akeman Street, now the A41. Britain's first Norman castle was built here by Robert de Mortain, half-brother to William I, and because of its strategic position the castle was used by royalty and nobles for several centuries; Thomas à Becket held it while Chancellor. Abandoned in the 15th century, and dismantled in the 16th, only the massive banks and ditches remain, with a stone keep.

The very long High Street, with several attractive period buildings on or in the narrow roads just behind it, forms the basis of the town, running for two miles along

the valley of the River Bulbourne, which it shares with both the Grand Union Canal, and the extremely busy London-to-Birmingham railway line. The topography of the valley ensures that the town remains confined, never more than a mile across.

The late Graham Greene, whose father was headmaster of the public school, was born here. The school was considerably expanded from a delightful Tudor grammar school during the 19th century. It is sited north of the restored Parish Church of St Peter, which contains a window dedicated to the poet, William Cowper, who was born in the rectory.

BETCHWORTH
MAP REF: 91TQ2150

A long, straggling village near Box Hill, Betchworth once possessed a castle, built during the 14th and 15th centuries beside the River Mole. Today the scant remains are covered by earth banks on a golf course. The village has a number of interesting buildings, including

three 16th-century timber-framed cottages, the Dolphin Inn (c.1700) and More Place, a 15th-century house with grounds sloping to the river.

The medieval Church of St Michael is of interest because its tower is at the south end – placed there when the Norman tower became unstable and was replaced during extensive 19th-century restoration work. Inside the church there is a chest, said to have been carved from an oak tree that was growing before the birth of Christ.

The use of lime was a vital factor in early agriculture and the remains of lime quarries scar the North Downs. Some of the largest remains of lime kilns can still be seen in the old quarries above Betchworth and Brockham.

Brockham is famous for its triangular green on which W G Grace is just one of the famous cricketers to have played. There are some good houses and cottages around the green and fine views of Box Hill. The carefully placed Victorian church completes a picturesque scene.

BISHOP'S STORTFORD
MAP REF: 89TL4821

On the border, and more Essex than Hertfordshire, this busy market town developed in the 18th century as a coaching station between London, Newmarket and Norwich. The commercial viability of the town improved once the River Stour was made navigable in 1789. Its major industry was malting – Hertfordshire had some 80 maltings in the mid 19th century – and several of the original buildings survive, and, although converted, they are quite distinctive.

William the Conqueror built Waytemore Castle here, granting it to the Norman Bishops of London. The castle was largely destroyed by King John and the four-acre space it occupied is now a park, containing only traces of the central mound of the castle. One of the town's most notable buildings, the 19th-century corn exchange, occupies half of the original market place but it has now been converted into shops and offices. Several pleasing coaching inns remain and Tissiman's timber-framed shop in the High Street is eye-catching. Cecil Rhodes' father was vicar here, and Cecil was born in the old vicarage, now the Rhodes Memorial Museum, in South Street.

The Grand Union Canal follows the valley of the River Bulbourne through Berkhamsted on its way north to Birmingham from London ▼

▲ Winter at Burnham Beeches, where several of the huge beech trees are well over 300 years old

BURNHAM BEECHES
MAP REF: 86SU9584

Some 400 acres of this magnificent stretch of ancient Chiltern beechwood and common have been owned and maintained by the Corporation of London since 1879. A notable recreation area, Burnham Beeches was extended in 1921 when the first Viscount Burnham gave 88 acres of Fleet Wood. There are six miles of forest drives and numerous paths and bridleways.

At their colourful peak in the autumn, the majestic beech trees – some up to 400 years old – dominate the woodlands they share with oak, silver birch, holly and rhododendrons. In the early Middle Ages this area was scrub and common, but it avoided enclosure and developed as woodland. Between the 16th and 19th centuries many trees were pollarded to produce poles, firewood and animal fodder, and their weird shapes are a result of this action. Fallow and the secretive muntjac deer live in the woods, while squirrels and jays feed on the beechmast. Woodpeckers, tree-creepers, owls and tits are all common in an area containing a prolific number of bird species.

CHALFONT ST GILES
MAP REF: 86SU9893

In 1665, old and blind, John Milton left London to escape the Plague and lived in a cottage in Chalfont St Giles until the following year. During that period he completed *Paradise Lost* and began *Paradise Regained*. The cottage is now a museum containing relics of the poet. Chalfont is a pretty place, with half-timbered cottages and the parish church, with its medieval wall paintings, clustered by a green.

Near by, the **Chiltern Open Air Museum** displays vernacular buildings, mostly from the area, although the painstakingly rebuilt, early 16th-century cruck-framed barn is from Arborfield, near Reading. There are a number of barns, a baker's granary from Wing, a smith's forge and even a Victorian privy. A more ambitious project is the Victorian furniture factory from High Wycombe, where the tollhouse was also originally located. The museum has Iron Age reconstructions, based on archaeological evidence, and a fine nature trail.

CHARTWELL
MAP REF: 93TQ4551

Sir Winston Churchill and his family lived here from 1924 until his death 40 years later. The house stands on the slope of a steep-sided valley and, until the destructive storms of the late 1980s, the slopes facing the house were heavily wooded. The National Trust has planted some 7,000 trees, but the site is, at present, very exposed. Chartwell was largely rebuilt by Philip Tilden for Churchill, producing a pleasant house of no great architectural merit, but immense atmosphere. Light, airy rooms look out over the gardens Churchill redesigned to emphasise the different levels, adding terraces and walls – he was justly proud of his skill as a bricklayer – ponds and lakes.

One of the lakes is home to the descendants of the black Australian swans Churchill introduced to Chartwell, while inside the house

The 16th-century cottage at Chalfont St Giles in which Milton lived ▼

there are, naturally, many reminders of the statesman. It is beautifully and lovingly maintained. Several rooms, including his wonderful study, are much as they were when he died, while the guest rooms have been converted to a museum containing more weighty mementoes.

Churchill was a talented painter and some of his own paintings adorn the walls of the house. In the garden, visitors can walk into his studio, where he worked, and

in 1627, retaining Chenies until the 1950s, and continuing to be buried in the chapel (rarely open) attached to the parish church.

Chenies village was largely rebuilt in the last century when the Bedfords were leaders of the fashion for landlords to implement wholesale 'improvements' to their holdings. In Tudor revival style, the cottages are set around a sloping green, creating a picturesque, yet not entirely convincing, effect.

Chenies Manor. The garden features an unusual Physick Garden where herbs are grown for medicinal and culinary use, as well as for perfume ▼

which contains many examples of his work. Casually placed near one of the ponds is Churchill's canvas chair, waiting for him to arrive to feed the fish.

CHENIES
MAP REF: 87TQ0198

The Russell family, later Earls and Dukes of Bedford, acquired the manor of Isenhamsted Chenies in the 16th century and began to extend the charming Early English brick-built manor house. The west wing contains the tower, built in about 1460, and the south wing with its Tudor chimneys similar to those at Hampton Court, notable staircase, long gallery and other rooms was added by the 1st Earl of Bedford primarily to entertain Henry VIII. It is said that Catherine Howard committed adultery with Thomas Culpeper here; the steps of a lame man – the King – are sometimes heard making his way to her room. The Russells moved to Woburn Abbey

CHESSINGTON
MAP REF: 91TQ1863

In the 1940s Chessington Zoo had the rather daring idea of adding a special attraction for children, and introduced a Ghost Train. Nowadays, more than 100 attractions have been added, ranging from a replica of an Olde English Market Square and an American frontier town to a monorail giving panoramic views of the zoo. There is a circus which, following modern trends, does not use animal acts, and a fun fair which uses the most modern fairground technology. All this has led to the re-naming of the site World of Adventures and the success of these 'extras' can be judged by the often jammed roads leading to Chessington at weekends.

Happily, the zoo continues to flourish, maintaining a wide variety of animals, birds and reptiles. Should London Zoo close, Chessington will be left as the only zoo in the Greater London area.

CHIDDINGSTONE
MAP REF: 93TQ5045

This wonderfully attractive place is everyone's idea of an 'olde worlde' English village and, unlike many claiming that distinction, it is genuine. At its centre a row of unspoilt 16th- and 17th-century houses, complete with magnificent inn, face a 17th-century church, its raised graveyard sheltered by trees. Some of the houses are half-timbered with classic Wealden black-and-white overhanging upper storeys; others, including the inn, are timber-framed and brick. Some may incorporate even older buildings – the village shop and post office is mentioned in a 15th-century deed. Just outside the village is the castle, basically a rather simple 17th-century manor house given 19th-century Gothick additions. The village, but not the castle, is owned by the National Trust.

Chiddingstone was a product of the iron industry which flourished in the Weald of Kent during the 16th and 17th centuries. The medieval manor which the castle replaced was the seat of the local ironmasters, the Streatfeild family. The castle retains paintings of the family but was acquired in the 1950s by Denys Eyre Bower, one of that remarkable breed of collectors who seem to occur in each century. Originally a bank employee in Derbyshire, he became a London antiques dealer and filled the castle with a heady mixture of Stuart and Jacobite relics and ancient Egyptian and Japanese art.

CHINNOR
MAP REF: 86SP7501

A village dominated by a cement works would not appear the obvious choice for inclusion here, but Chinnor's 13th-century Church of St Andrew has a very large collection of contemporary brasses and important, and charming, 14th-century stained glass. Unusually, it also possesses several oil paintings thought to be by Sir James Thornhill, whose work in the dome of St Paul's and the Painted Hall at Greenwich made him the foremost and most honoured artist of his day.

Chinnor Hill lies south-east of the village at the crossing of the Icknield Way and the Ridgeway. A 70-acre nature reserve on the Ridgeway contains wood and grassland and is home to many species of birds and wild flowers, including frog orchid.

CHISWICK

MAP REF: 92TQ2078

Chiswick Reach is a beautiful and historic stretch of the River Thames west of Hammersmith Bridge. Chiswick Mall and Strand on the Green have Restoration and Georgian houses while the 18th-century Chiswick House is one of the finest Palladian houses in Britain. Designed by Richard Boyle, 3rd Earl of Burlington, and William Kent, as 'a pavilion of the spirit' to house Burlington's library and art collection, it has interiors by Kent, who also designed the Italianate gardens.

William Hogarth is buried in Chiswick churchyard, and Hogarth House, hard by Chiswick flyover, still has the mulberry tree which yielded fruit for his wife's tarts, made for the foundling hospital whose inmates her husband used for his models. Today it is almost impossible to comprehend that Hogarth House was a country home. Indeed, less than a century before Burlington, Hogarth and others made Chiswick a cultural centre, the area was known mainly for producing baskets made from osiers harvested along the Thames – how things have changed!

CLANDON PARK

MAP REF: 91TQ0351

The Venetian architect Giacomo Leoni built this imposing house for the 2nd Lord Onslow in the early 1730s. Inside, one of the most notable features is the two-storey baroque marble hall. The house has been little altered, and contains fine 18th-century rooms, decorated with superb plasterwork. Many of the Onslows have followed parliamentary careers, three becoming Speaker of the House of Commons; their portraits are in the Speaker's Parlour with the 'vinegar' bible, so named because of a misprint in the parable of the vineyard.

In 1968 the National Trust acquired the Gubbay collection of furniture, textiles, carpets and richly coloured Chinese porcelain birds. As few of the original contents remained at Clandon, the Trust transferred the collection to the house.

Sited incongruously in the gardens is a Maori meeting house, brought to Clandon by the 4th Earl when he completed a term as Governor of New Zealand in 1892 (see page 78).

CLAREMONT LANDSCAPE GARDEN AND HOUSE

MAP REF: 92SU1464

Claremont is the earliest surviving example of an English landscape garden, worked on by several of the great names in gardening design, yet it had been derelict for many years until the National Trust restored it in the mid 1970s. It has a three-acre amphitheatre where events are held during the summer.

The lake is shallow but holds many fish and is home to a number of species of wildfowl – some introduced – and other water birds including, some years ago, a young osprey. The garden has several ornamental buildings, among them a pavilion on the island in the centre of the lake and a grotto beside the lake. The oldest feature is the belvedere tower designed by Vanbrugh who also built the original house on the site. When Clive of India purchased the estate in 1768, he decided to replace it and commissioned Capability Brown and Henry Holland to design and build a house in Palladian style; naturally Brown also extended the gardens. From 1816 to 1922, Claremont was a royal residence and Queen Victoria stayed in it both as a child and in the early years of her reign. The house has been a private girls' school for many years and is not open (see page 75).

CLAYDON HOUSE

MAP REF: 86SP7226

The Verney family has lived at Claydon since 1620. The original Jacobean mansion was demolished in the 18th century by the 2nd Earl who built the classical west wing and then, encouraged by Sir Thomas Robinson, an amateur architect, began extending the house. Robinson's grandiose scheme bankrupted Verney before the work was complete and the additions were later removed, leaving only the west wing – and no proper front door.

Inside, the interior decorations are eccentric but breathtaking and unequalled. The most remarkable are those fashioned in wood from the fantastic imagination of one Luke Lightfoot, a wood-carver of genius. His rooms are the north hall and pink parlour on the ground floor and the Gothic room, paper room and Chinese room – the high point of the cult of chinoiserie – on the first floor. In contrast, the rooms decorated by the stuccoist, Joseph Rose, appear positively restrained, but where his talents combine with those of Robinson the result is quite outstanding (see page 77).

CLIVEDEN

MAP REF: 86SU9185

Now a luxury hotel, this is the third house on this magnificent site, 200ft above the Thames. Built by Sir Charles Barry for the Duke of Sutherland, it was added to by both the Duke of Westminster and the Astor family at the end of the 19th century. The Astors and their friends formed the Cliveden Set in the 1930s, when Nancy, Lady Astor lived here.

The glorious grounds, with walks through superb beech woodland, stretch down to Cliveden Reach on the Thames, a silvery ribbon far below the house. The National Trust opens the gardens, including the enchanting rose garden, and a

◄ Clandon Park. The house, but not the park, is owned by the National Trust

▲ The Statue of Love at Cliveden

water garden with giant carp and Chinese pagoda. The formal parterre below the terrace is linked to it by the Borghese balustrade, brought here from Rome by the 1st Viscount Astor. Two delightful garden buildings by Leoni are worth seeking out, as is the view of the Thames from Canning's Oak. Three rooms in the hotel are opened to the public (see page 77).

COBHAM
MAP REF: 89TQ6768

Cobham is now a conservation area and contains many fine buildings. Most of the village houses are 18th-century but an earlier, and celebrated, survival is the half-timbered inn, the Leather Bottle, immensely popular with tourists both because of its age and its connections with Dickens' *Pickwick Papers*.

In 1362 Sir John de Cobham founded Cobham College, south of the Church of St Mary Magdalene, as a chantry for five priests. The buildings were converted to almshouses in the late 16th century and a courtyard is open to the public each afternoon. The church boasts a unique collection of 17 superbly detailed medieval brasses (see Monuments and Memorials, page 61).

The Cobham family seat, **Cobham Hall**, is a very large Elizabethan redbrick manor house in parkland later laid out by Humphry Repton. Now a girls' public school, the house is open on certain days in the spring and summer. Inside it is a bewildering mixture of styles with work by Wyatt and Repton. The park, a favourite walking place of Dickens, retains some beautiful trees.

The village possesses one more good building in **Owletts**, another redbrick house, but a century or so later than Cobham Hall. It has a contemporary staircase under an ornate plaster ceiling, and a clock showing the time in all parts of the Empire. Much of the present interior furnishings, like the clock, were introduced by Sir Herbert Baker, Lutyens' associate in the design of New Delhi.

Cobham's Leather Bottle inn is famous for its associations with Charles Dickens. Appropriate prints hang inside ▼

COMPTON
MAP REF: 90SU9546

This sprawling, but charming, village houses two remarkable buildings. When the Victorian artist G F Watts died, his wife Mary designed the Arts and Crafts mortuary chapel in which he is buried. The outside of this incredible building has been compared to a red London bus loitering against the green of the Surrey hills, and the inside is the supreme monument to art nouveau. Near by is the Watts Gallery, displaying 200 of his works.

St Nicholas' Church is very important, combining Saxon and early 11th-century work with a unique 12th-century two-storeyed sanctuary, a chapel above a low, vaulted chamber. Three unexpected little dormer windows beside the Saxon tower, itself topped by a small spire, give the church a very appealing appearance, while two magnificent cedars protect it. Inside, the east window has some early 13th-century stained glass. Canterbury, Lincoln and York have glass of this age, but few parish churches can equal it.

▲ Cygnets tied up prior to having their beaks notched

SWAN-UPPING

The annual voyage along the Thames to 'up' the swans from the water and mark the beaks of the cygnets has been going on since Elizabeth I's time. Swans have been royal birds since the Middle Ages, when the penalties for killing one or taking an egg were ferocious. All swans on open water belong to the Queen, except for some on the Thames which by ancient tradition are owned by two of the London livery companies, the Vintners and the Dyers.

The ritual of swan-upping begins in the third week of July, when the royal Keeper of Swans, accompanied by the Swan Markers of the two livery companies, sets off in a procession of rowing skiffs from Sunbury to journey up the Thames as far as Pangbourne. Until 1980 the voyage started at Southwark Bridge in the City. The oarsmen wear colourful livery and the boats fly flags and banners.

It takes four days to examine all the swan families on the river, haul them into the boats – which takes considerable skill and experience – and inspect their beaks. If the parent swans belong to the Vintners, two nicks are cut in each cygnet's beak. The Dyers' cygnets are marked with a single notch, while the Queen's cygnets go unmarked. If a brood is the product of a mixed alliance, complicated rules come into play to determine how many of the cygnets are allotted to each strain in their ancestry.

The Vintners and the Dyers still serve roast swan as the high point of an elaborate ceremonial banquet every year.

One of the official Swan Markers who accompany the Swan Keeper on the procession along the river ▼

▲ Messing about in boats is a popular pastime at Cookham

MAP REF: 86SU8985

A pretty village beside the Thames, celebrated for its most famous 'son', the 20th-century artist Stanley Spencer, and for the ritual of swan-upping, the theme of one of Spencer's most famous paintings now in the Tate Gallery. Spencer was born in 1891 in a tall semi-detached house in the attractive High Street. Near by the Stanley Spencer Gallery was founded after he died in 1959 and contains some of his work, much of it depicting events in the Bible using local scenes and people.

The village green at **Cookham Dean**, with several acres of common and woodland, belong to the National Trust. Combined with a group of farms to the south the result is a protective cloak around Cookham, successfully guarding it against over-development. Indeed, the village is something of a rarity; it remains a place where modern buildings do not intrude on the pleasing vernacular architecture of many centuries.

At **Bisham**, on the other side of the A404, there is an abbey said to be haunted by the ghost of Lady Elizabeth Hoby. Her tomb can be seen in the village church.

MAP REF: 86SP7610

John Bigge, whom some allege to have been the executioner of Charles I, spent the last years of his life as a hermit in the countryside around Dinton. Bigge had been secretary to Simon Mayne of Dinton Hall, one of those who signed the King's death warrant. Found guilty of regicide, Mayne died in the Tower in 1661.

There is a memorial brass to an earlier Simon Mayne in the Church of St Peter and St Paul. On the tympanum – the area between the door lintel and the arch above it – a very large dragon attacks a very small St Michael who is armed only with a cross.

Nearby **Westlington** has some charming old cottages.

MAP REF: 91TQ1649

The High Street of this pleasant market town has several good old buildings but they need to be sought out, since some have been camouflaged by later additions. The White Horse Inn is an example; parts are thought to be 15th-century, but the front is later. Good vernacular architecture is represented by Pixham Mill and Castle Mill on the River Mole just east of the town. Both these privately owned 19th-century mills can be viewed from passing footpaths. Dorking has been considerably more successful than some towns in combining old and new architecture, and its new council offices demonstrate good modern practice.

The Victorian Church of St Martin may dominate the town by virtue of possessing one of the highest spires in all England, but it is the hills which truly command Dorking. South of the town, **Leith Hill** is the highest point in south-east England; from the tower on its top there are said to be views of 12 counties. To the north, **Box Hill** continues to attract vast numbers on public holidays, as it has for two centuries – the National Trust is facing a constant battle against erosion of the paths. The most exciting route to the top is the Zig Zag road from Mickleham, often impassable in winter. The views from Box Hill's steep chalk slopes are vast, extending over the Weald to the South Downs. Below, the quiet River Mole can be glimpsed, almost unbelievably the architect of the great cutting in which Dorking lies. The box tree continues to grow here and orchids survive on the grassland, now regularly cropped by sheep. The beech woods behind are pleasantly cool on the hottest day but, for those seeking a quieter alternative, the more open and sandy **Headley Common** is just a mile or so north.

DORNEY COURT
MAP REF: 90SU9378

Dorney Court has been described as being one of the finest Tudor manor houses in England and it is a most delightful place – from the outside all mellow redbrick and timber. It has been owned by the Palmer family for more than 400 years and they have acquired much beautiful furniture over the centuries which adds further lustre to the fine rooms open to the public. The best of these are, perhaps, the parlour and the great hall with its linenfold panelling and family portraits. There is a long tradition that the first pineapple to be raised in England was grown here and presented to King Charles II – it is commemorated by a carving of the fruit in the hall.

The village church contains a wall painting of the Annunciation, but the main feature is the remarkable tomb of the Garrard family. Sir William and his wife kneel, facing each other, attended by their 15 children, five of whom carry skulls, indicating that they died before their parents.

A final, brief, visit should be made to the Hermitage, a cottage ornée of stone and flint.

DUNMOW, GREAT & LITTLE
MAP REF: 89TL6222

The ceremony of the Dunmow Flitch appears to date from the founding of a priory at Little Dunmow in the early years of the 12th century. Each year the prior awarded a side, or flitch, of bacon to a couple who could best demonstrate their fidelity and harmony. This happy-go-lucky ceremony disappeared in the 18th century but has been revived, in somewhat different form, and moved to Great Dunmow. Doctor's Pond provides Great Dunmow's other claim to fame, for it was here that the first experiments with a self-righting lifeboat were carried out by Lionel Lukin.

Little Dunmow church consists of the south aisle of the old priory and contains a chair, said, doubtfully, to be that in which early winners of the Flitch were transported round the village. Apart from this, the villages are quietly pretty in a way many Essex villages are, unassuming and enjoyable.

DUNSTABLE
MAP REF: 87TL0122

The Romans and the Saxons attempted to establish a settlement at this point on the Icknield Way, but the market town of Dunstable was created by Henry I. It remained small, though gaining in importance when the coach trade developed along Watling Street, and when the local craft of straw-plaiting led to the establishment of hat-making as an industry. The coming of the railways concentrated hat-making in Luton but expansion of the printing and engineering industries resulted in the expansion of Dunstable early in this century.

Dunstable is relatively rich in old buildings, with almshouses, old schools – there was a school here in the 12th century – and several 16th- and 17th-century inns, nowadays sometimes in different guise. The town also has a number of modern buildings, by no means all supporting the fashionable belief that modern equals poor!

South of the town lies the chalk ridge of **Dunstable Downs**, which was acquired piecemeal by the National Trust over a period of some 20 years. Neglected, the land had reverted to scrub but, by fencing and grazing, the area is once again 'unimproved' arable land and many typical downland plants have re-established themselves, as has the small blue butterfly. The views to the west from the triangulation point take in the whole of the Vale of Aylesbury.

▲ St Peter's in Dunstable retains the nave of the priory, founded in 1131

groups of prehistoric burial mounds in Britain can be seen at **Five Knolls**, on the downs. The group includes bowl, bell and pond barrows. The most northerly of the two bowl barrows was excavated by Sir Mortimer Wheeler in the late 1920s and yielded a female buried in a crouched position, with a later cremation. A further 30 bodies, probably the victims of murder, were added in Saxon times.

EAST GRINSTEAD

MAP REF: 93TQ3938

The arrival of the railway led East Grinstead to expand, and it now has a large dormitory population housed in post-war estates. However, the centre retains a pleasant country town appearance, with many attractive older buildings, particularly along the High Street. The almshouse known as Sackville College is the finest building in the town, dated 1609 but founded two years earlier. Its low stone front, with gables and tall chimneys, is pleasing, but the quadrangle behind would not be out of place in Oxford or Cambridge; the hall and Victorian chapel can be visited. The Warden who commissioned the chapel wrote that popular carol, 'Good King Wenceslas'.

Amherst House and Cromwell House, opposite the college, are among several timber-framed houses of the 15th and 16th centuries to be seen, a reminder that this is Wealden country. The iron grave-slabs in the churchyard of St Swithun's also confirm that the iron industry once flourished here. The Queen Victoria Hospital, on the outskirts of the town, established its world-wide reputation for plastic surgery during World War II, under the pioneering surgeon, Sir Archibald McIndoe.

Ashdown Forest, south of the town, resembles the New Forest in that it is now more heath than woodland. The Forest Way Country Park has been created from some nine miles of the old East Grinstead, Groombridge and Tunbridge Wells Railway. Suitable for walkers, cyclists and, in part, wheelchair users, it is home to a wide variety of plant and animal life. For Standen, see page 66.

EATON BRAY

MAP REF: 86SP9720

Always expect the unexpected when exploring England. An example is the link between the church at Eaton Bray and Westminster Abbey. The marvellous scrolled ironwork on the south door of St Mary's is by Thomas of Leighton, responsible for the railings around the tomb of Queen Eleanor in the Abbey. There are other surprises, for the interior has some of the finest 13th-century carvings and mouldings to be found on the arches of any church in the country.

The village of Eaton Bray is some

▲ Sackville College was originally built by Robert Sackville to house 21 men and 10 unmarried women who had been servants at Knole

two miles long, containing almost every type of building – stone, brick, timber, thatch – interspersed with orchards. There has been a degree of infilling, but there are a number of attractive buildings to be discovered. The street known as the Rye is interesting, as are the three pubs and a well-preserved mill at the south end of the village.

EPPING FOREST

MAP REF: 88TQ3997

Epping Forest is a remnant of the ancient Royal Forest of Essex and once extended to at least 60,000 acres. Nowadays it covers a mere 6,000 acres, lying mainly on either side of the A104. The Forest still contains open spaces, a reminder of the days when much was commonland, but it also possesses a large number of fine native trees including oak, beech and hornbeam. The centuries-long practice of pollarding is reflected in the distorted shapes the trees, particularly the hornbeam, have developed since the beginning of this century when pollarding ceased – wrongly, in the view of many experts.

The Forest has been freely open to the public since the passing of the Epping Forest Act of 1878 stopped encroachment and handed control to the Corporation of the City of London. This essential action established the Forest as the main area where East Enders could escape and relax from the problems of life in London. Two long-distance footpaths, the Essex Way and the Forest Way, begin in the Forest, which is criss-crossed with bridleways; one of the best ways to discover the Forest is to hire a horse. There is a conservation centre at **High Beach** which provides a trail guide in addition to giving details of the natural history of the area. Queen Elizabeth's Hunting Lodge – a timber-framed building for viewing the hunt built for Henry VIII – at **Chingford** has displays covering the history of the Forest, including details of the Iron Age fort at **Ambresbury Banks**, a mile south of Epping. Romantic folklore claims this as the site where Boudicca was defeated by the Romans and took her own life.

Well-laid-out paths weave through the ancient trees of Epping Forest ▼

Eton College, England's largest and arguably most prestigious school for boys. The buildings occupy a large part of the small town ▶

The completion of the M11 and M25 has rather isolated the town of **Epping**, which was once a resting place on the highway from London to East Anglia via Newmarket and Thetford. Yet the town has character, with several inns that reflect its coaching past. One of the most interesting buildings is the castellated redbrick water-tower of 1872 – a typical Victorian conceit.

EPSOM
MAP REF: 91TQ2160

Epsom owes its development as a spa to the discovery of spring water containing sulphate of magnesium on Epsom Common during the 17th century, and its popularity was enhanced by the beginning, shortly after, of racing on the Downs above the town. By the end of the 18th century the popularity of the town as a spa had declined, but the quality of its roads had dramatically improved and Epsom was established as an 'in' place for City merchants.

The town has suffered in recent years from redevelopment, but it is still possible to find some of the fine houses built at that time in Church Street, South Street and at Woodcote. Many of the older buildings have been adapted – the first assembly rooms in the world were in Waterloo House, now hidden behind the modern front of a building society. The original well has survived and can be found, signposted The Wells, off the A24 between Epsom and Ashtead. The busy High Street – Epsom has no bypass – is a combination of modern and older buildings. Its centre is taken over by a market on Saturdays.

The Derby is the most famous horse race in the world, often copied but never emulated. Run over a difficult, undulating course, allegedly too early in the season, it invariably reveals the best horse of each generation! Proximity to London and the arrival of the railway in the 1850s ensured huge attendances for the big race; Frith's famous 1858 painting of *Derby Day*, in the Tate, is a marvellous record of a social occasion. Television coverage now boosts the annual audience to many millions, and Epsom becomes the focus of the racing world for one day each June.

ETON
MAP REF: 90SU9677

Eton is linked to the town of Windsor (see page 73) by an early 19th-century iron bridge. The life of the town revolves round the school, much enlarged from that founded in 1440 by Henry VI, when he was only 19. Originally intended for the education of '70 poor scholars', Eton has been increasingly patronised by the well-born, privileged and wealthy, and has played a pivotal role in all walks of British public life. No other school approaches Eton in the numbers of old boys who have occupied senior posts in Government, the City and Industry. At holiday times – the ideal time to discover the charms of the town – parts of the school are open to visitors who can inspect the names carved on desks and panelling by famous scholars of the past.

▲ During term time boys and masters are a familiar sight in Eton

Henry intended Eton College chapel to be the choir of a vast church he planned to build next to the school but he was deposed in 1461 and the rest of the project was abandoned. The chapel ranks as one of the finest Perpendicular buildings in England. Inside, the 15th-century wall paintings, generally agreed to be the best in northern Europe, were covered over, by the college barber, at the Reformation. Rediscovered by the Victorians, they were, unbelievably, concealed again, but in 1923 they were 'rescued' and now add immeasurably to the beauty of the chapel.

EWHURST
MAP REF: 91TQ0940

William Cobbett thought Ewhurst a very pretty village and, as he gave praise sparingly, it is worth studying. To gain an overall view the visitor should climb Pitch Hill, about a mile north, from where it is possible to see the three straggling sections comprising the village. Furthest from the hill is the green, then the church and, nearest, a cluster of cottages. In addition, there are a number of late Victorian houses hidden among the trees on the slopes of Pitch Hill – important to students of architecture, they add little to the charm of the village.

The separation of green and church suggests that the centre of the village has shifted over the centuries; certainly most of the more attractive houses and cottages are in the north part of the village. Some are timber-framed and several have unusual fish-tail pattern tiles.

Much of the local forest and commonland is administered by a voluntary organisation, Hurtwood Control, responsible for guaranteeing public access. At the village of **Hurtwood** is Ewhurst windmill, once a smugglers' haunt, now converted to a private house. Near by, **Coverwood Lakes** are open occasionally in May and June. Slowly recovering from the disastrous 1987 storms, this is a charming garden containing many bog and water plants encouraged by the naturally damp conditions around the four lakes. The spring shows of azaleas and rhododendrons are particularly pleasing.

FARNHAM

MAP REF: 90SU8346

Farnham's early development was aided by its position on one of England's oldest highways, between its two capitals – Winchester and London. Today the town is bypassed, but the long main street, with offshoots down to church and river and up to the castle standing 'nobly on a hill', follows the line of the old road.

For centuries the castle was owned by the Bishops of Winchester who already held Farnham and vast estates around it at the time of Domesday. It passed to the See of Guildford in 1927, ceasing to be the Bishop's residence in 1956. During the troubled medieval period the castle was used by the bishops to entertain many royal guests. Occupied by both sides in the Civil War it was slighted but repaired and the domestic buildings, including the remarkable 15th-century brick Waynflete Tower, are still in use. English Heritage open the 12th-century keep to the public.

Wool, cloth manufacture, wheat (Farnham had the largest corn market in England, outside London, according to Defoe), pottery and hops have all contributed to the prosperity Farnham displays with grace and charm. Castle Hill contains some of the grandest Georgian houses to be found in the south-east, while wide Castle Street is full of more fine Georgian and Victorian buildings, interspersed with older, timber-framed houses.

Willmer House, in West Street, a splendid, early Georgian house with a fine staircase and lovely walled garden, is the town museum. The cobbled Lower Church Lane leads to the Parish Church of St Andrew between rows of charming brick cottages, and Church Lane, by the churchyard, has a pleasing variety of bigger houses. Intelligent modern developments, art galleries and a theatre add to the appeal – even the acerbic William Cobbett, born and buried in Farnham, would surely still approve of his town and, particularly of the re-naming of his birthplace, a pub, after him!

FARNINGHAM

MAP REF: 89TQ5467

Farningham lies in the shadow of the M20, the second major road to bypass it, as the parallel A20 has long been diverted away from its narrow, charming main street. There are several interesting houses in the village, the most important undoubtedly being the mill complex beside the Darent at the west of the village. Though not open, the white weatherboarded watermill and fine mill house can be seen from near the small hump-backed brick bridge (1773) over the river. Almost opposite is the attractive Lion Inn, facing the bridge.

The ford by the inn at Farningham has been closed to traffic, but that at **Eynsford** remains, the road from it leading to the Roman Villa at Lullingstone (see page 59). Eynsford has many pretty half-timbered buildings, an interesting church, a large viaduct and the remains of an important small 12th-century castle. One of the earliest to be built of stone, its curtain wall is well preserved, rising to some 30ft. Parts of the undercroft of the hall and the solar can also be seen.

Next, going south, is **Shoreham**, containing even more vernacular buildings of various ages. The centre of the village is particularly attractive. William Blake often stayed with the painter Samuel Palmer who lived here for some years, and the bulk of his scenes, including many with a biblical theme, depict the Darent valley, described by Palmer as his 'Valley of Vision'.

Finally, the most southerly village, and now the largest, is **Otford**, possessor of a unique listed building, the 11th-century village pond! The High Street has several pleasant houses of various ages and in a meadow by the river are the remains of the, once very large, Archbishop Warham's Palace, partially converted into cottages.

FELSTED

MAP REF: 89TL6720

Richard Rich was clearly both a good administrator and a sound politician who served two kings and various masters, surviving by a combination of ruthlessness and good fortune! He was Speaker of the Commons and later, as Chancellor, acquired various properties in Essex. In 1564 he founded Felsted School, one of literally hundreds of schools privately endowed between 1550 and 1660. This famous school had its beginnings in one room, the upper storey of a timber-framed building standing in front of the church.

There is a remarkable memorial in the Church of Holy Cross to Baron Rich. He died four years after founding the school but it was not until 1620 that the 15ft marble monument was built, by his grandson. It depicts Rich and his son in front of a tableau of the great man communicating with various of the Virtues.

Today, Felsted has a vineyard, Felstar, producing English wine. It offers tours for groups, and wine tastings.

FRENSHAM

MAP REF: 90SU8540

Frensham Ponds belong to the National Trust and a large area around them is now a country park. The district consists of sandy heath with scant woodlands, although silver birch has required control in recent years, and gorse and heather provide colour and cover for a wide range of bird and animal species. In winter the ponds attract bird rarities including the osprey first reported by Gilbert White in 1773.

Fishing and sailing are permitted here, but Frensham faces problems from over-use as areas around the ponds suffer badly from erosion. The Great Pond was originally a fish pond for the monks of Winchester – it has been estimated that the Church's estates around Farnham may have covered 25,000 acres when Domesday was compiled.

There is a group of four bowl barrows on a hill between the Ponds and, to the south, three

Harvest time at the vineyard at Felsted, where white wine is produced ▼

NAMES AND PLACES

Place name experts are more cautious than they used to be and it is generally accepted that the meanings are frequently no more than guesswork. The great majority of place names in the area around London are Old English in origin, as a result of the occupation of the region by the Anglo-Saxons after the withdrawal of the Roman army. A few older Celtic names have survived, however, notably that of the Thames, which may mean 'dark'. Wendover is another ancient British name, meaning 'white river' and referring to the chalky bed of the stream there.

Curiously named Friday Street near Leith Hill in Surrey ▼

Many names are related to natural features. Fords across rivers account for names like Chelmsford, Romford, Dartford and Guildford. Names ending in -hurst, such as Goudhurst, are from an Old English word for a wooded hill. Chart, which crops up often in Kent refers to heathland. Tring is a shortening of Trehanger, 'tree slope'. Various vague Old English terms for a house, a village, a farmstead, lie behind names ending in -ton, -ham and -worth.

Things are not always what they seem, however. Edenbridge has a bridge over the River Eden, but is thought to owe its name to a Saxon landowner named Eadhelm who built the bridge to begin with. A name ending in -ley normally refers to a meadow or clearing, as in Crawley and Cranleigh, but Camberley was coined by a local doctor when the railway came through in 1877, to make a classier impression than the earlier Cambridge Town. Bagshot and Marlow are both of uncertain significance, and Billericay is beyond all conjecture.

Some euphonious names were created in the Middle Ages by adding the landowner's name to that of the village. Hence Stoke Poges and Aston Clinton, Chesham Bois and Weston Turville, Shellow Bowells, Willingdale Doe and Willingdale Spain, Theydon Bois and Theydon Garnon. Princes Risborough belonged to the Black Prince. The owner of Farnham Royal had the duty of supporting the king's arm at the coronation.

Some names are engagingly odd. Easter in High Easter and Good Easter, in Essex, is said to mean a sheepfold. Christmas Pie in Surrey seems to come from a local farming family there named Christmas, though there is a fanciful story about a baker, Mr Christmas, who made enormous pies, 5ft round. Friday Street may have been called that because it was a poor place, Friday being an unlucky day (because of the Crucifixion).

Some names are of recent coinage. Coryton in Essex is named after the Cory Brothers, who founded an oil refinery there in 1922. It was formerly Kynochtown, after Kynoch's munition works, which the Cory Brothers bought. On the other hand, nearby Shellhaven was called that long before the Shell oil refinery was built there. One must not jump too quickly to conclusions.

---

sandstone hillocks known as the Devil's Jumps. St Mary's Church at Frensham has a huge 14th-century tower but little else of interest except a large copper cauldron, said to have belonged to a famous local witch, Mother Ludlam.

GODALMING

MAP REF: 90SU9643

Godalming, like Farnham, is an old settlement, historically wealthy and situated on a major route. The town lies in a deep valley between steeply sloping wooded hills. Narrow roads lined with many interesting buildings create difficulties for traffic and encourage exploration on foot. Highlights include the old town hall, known as the Pepperpot, but only dating from 1814, and several 16th- and 17th-century houses and warehouses. The museum is sited in a 15th-century town house opposite the Pepperpot; it has displays related to local people, including Gertrude Jekyll. The most obvious feature of the church is its high, twisted, lead spire, unusual in this area.

▲ Tudor Courts in Godalming

The Wey Navigation, extending from the Thames through Guildford, ends at Godalming Wharf. On entering the town it passes the 18th-century bridge and the meadows known as Lammasland. A steep climb out of the town leads to Charterhouse School which moved here from Finsbury in 1885.

Winkworth Arboretum, south of the town, is full of fine trees and can be visited with great pleasure in both spring and autumn, while a mile or so west of the town is the hamlet of Eashing, with a fine medieval bridge over the Wey.

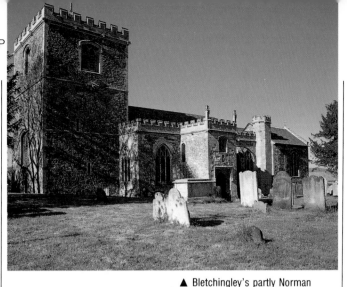

GODSTONE

MAP REF: 92TQ3551

Godstone is disposed around a large, square, tree-lined green with a small duck pond and a cricket pitch – the classic ingredients for an English village. Cottages and old inns frame the green, completing the picture.

A path leads from the White Hart Inn past **Bay Pond**, a nature reserve run by the Surrey Wildlife Trust. Once a hammer pond, it attracts many wildfowl during the winter, with passage birds in spring and autumn. The path continues to the parish church and a row of cottages known as Church Town. The almshouses are 19th-century and were built by George Gilbert Scott.

To the west of Godstone is **Bletchingley** which has one of the most attractive centres in Surrey. Once a prosperous market town, the village reflects this with many elegant buildings. The Whyte Harte Inn, mostly 16th-century, although said to incorporate earlier work, forms the centrepiece. Good timber-framed and tile-hung cottages can be found in Church Walk, once the old High Street. St Mary's Church, partly Norman, has a hermit's cell and superb views to the North Downs.

A mile north of the village, at

▲ Bletchingley's partly Norman church has a hermit's cell and medieval gargoyles

Brewer Street, is the 18th-century Place Farm, on the site of the mansion given to Anne of Cleves on her divorce from Henry VIII; only a Tudor gatehouse survives of her house. Brewer Street Farmhouse is a near-perfect 15th-century timber-framed hall house.

THE HOP-PICKING ARMY

Every year at the end of August an army of people (35,000 of them in the 1870s) used to descend like locusts on the green fields of Kent for the annual ritual of hop-picking. Whole families came, all ages from grandmothers to small children, for their annual hard-working country holiday. With them came gypsies and travelling folk in caravans and carts.

Special trains from the London stations carried the hop-picking horde to remote country stations which only came really alive this once in the year. Little single-track lines were constructed specially to meet the demand, like the 'Hop-Pickers' Line', which ran between Paddock Wood, east of Tonbridge, and Goudhurst. From the station beribboned farm carts took the pickers on to their final destinations.

Many families went to the same farm year after year, taking with them chairs, tables, beds and sometimes even wallpaper, which they would stick on the walls of their huts. The poorest families, unable to afford the train fare, would walk all the way from London, pushing the children in broken-down prams.

Preparations to receive the invaders began early. The village shops laid in provisions in heroic quantities – mountains of flour and sugar, and pyramids of cheeses – and carefully erected wire netting barricades in front of their counters to guard against pilfering or even outright assault. Farmers swept the huts out and piled up huge stacks of wood and kindling for the fires. The pickers were skilled open-air cooks and the writer Richard Church, who knew this part of the country well, described seeing the flames of their fires twinkling at night like the bivouac fires of an army.

Of an evening the pickers would repair to the local pub – where they were usually made to stay outside – for a drink and a cheerful singsong. Pickers would bring invalids and the elderly along with them because they had a firm faith in the healthfulness of the whole exercise and the powerful medicinal smell of the hops drying over fires in the kilns, which drifted across the countryside.

The tradition was still going strong after World War II, but now hop-picking has been completely mechanised. The little branch railway lines have all closed down and East Enders have more restful ways to spend a holiday.

Entire families journeyed to Kent for the annual hop-picking season ▼

GOUDHURST

MAP REF: 93TQ7237

One of a number of delightful Wealden villages, Goudhurst has the further advantage of a marvellously elevated position with breathtaking views across hop-fields, oast-houses, orchards and, to the west, parts of Sussex. The local claim is that from the belfry tower of St Mary's Church it is possible to see more than 50 other churches.

A row of weavers' cottages overlooks the churchyard, with more attractive cottages near the pond, at the end of which there is a weatherboarded building housing the local library. One of the three fine inns, the Star & Eagle, was used by members of the Hawkhurst Gang, who certainly did *not* conform to the image of smugglers as rather romantic fellows! One of their leaders, Kingsmill, a native of Goudhurst, threatened to burn the village to the ground when he learnt a local defence force had been set up. The gang attacked on 20 April 1747 but were driven off by a well-organised militia. Kingsmill was later hanged at Horsmonden.

On the outskirts of the village is Pattenden Manor (not open), a superbly maintained Wealden hall house of around 1470. At the foot of the hill is the entrance to **Finchcocks**, a rather grand country house of 1725, set in extensive parkland. Its owners have restored it and established a museum of keyboard instruments dating from the 17th century. Many are played during concerts at the house.

Kentish weatherboarding at Goudhurst ▼

Courses, fairs and children's events are also held here.

Due south of Goudhurst is the **Bedgebury National Pinetum.** Here, in 160 acres, waymarked paths lead between plantations of many different species of conifers planted by the Forestry Commission and the Royal Botanic Gardens. The trees, which also include various interesting deciduous varieties, are more colourful than one might suppose and cover two valleys. There is a lake too.

GRAVESEND

MAP REF: 93TQ6574

The Red Indian princess, Pocahontas, the first American Indian to visit England, died on board ship at Gravesend on her return journey to America in 1617. She is buried in the church and there is a statue to her in the churchyard. Pocahontas saved the life of John Smith, founder of Virginia, but later married another settler, believing Smith to be dead. Legend claims that she died of a broken heart when she discovered her mistake – legend is wrong, but there is something sad about her statue in so alien a setting.

The grim marshes so chillingly described by Dickens in *Great Expectations* lie to the east, while, out on the Thames, huge boats glide past, some bound for Tilbury, across the river, others heading for London. Gravesend has not lacked importance both as a dock and, for a period in the 19th century, as a resort – in the 1840s a million steamboat passengers arrived at its piers each year – while it is still the point on the Thames where the

river pilots board inbound vessels. The town suffered a serious fire in the 18th century and was largely rebuilt. Milton Chantry is the oldest surviving building. It has had a number of uses since it was built in the 14th century and English Heritage now run it as an arts centre.

Near by is the Fort, lived in and converted by the then Captain Gordon, later of Khartoum, when he was in charge of the Thames defences.

GREAT AMWELL

MAP REF: 88TL3712

If Eaton Bray (see page 42) can boast a connection with Westminster Abbey, then the Norman Church of St John the Baptist at Great Amwell can point to its link with old St Paul's! The 17th-century pulpit is said to have been fashioned from the sounding board of the original cathedral's pulpit. The church stands on a knoll and the sloping churchyard looks down, past yew and cypress, to the willow-fringed New River. The New is an artificial channel, created in the 17th century to carry fresh water to London. To commemorate this achievement, two islands were created just below the church. Man-made the scene may be, but it creates a most pleasurable effect.

GREAT COMP

MAP REF: 93TQ6457

Part of the pleasure of Great Comp is the knowledge that this beautiful garden has been created and brought to maturity in less than 40 years. When Mr and Mrs Roderick Cameron began their task, they had a 17th-century house with an Edwardian garden, and paddock and woodland covering some four-and-a-half acres. The garden has been extended to seven acres and the Camerons have achieved a series of linked areas with lawns, paving, semi-wooded walks, old and new walls and stone terraces and cleverly planned vistas. The careful mixture of deciduous and evergreen species – there are over 3,000 named plants – ensures that there is interest in the garden at all seasons (see page 75).

Great Comp is set on the northern edge of **Mereworth Woods** where there are paths and rides. Small areas of the woods may date back to the great Wealden forest that once stretched from Canterbury to Winchester.

GREENSTED-JUXTA-ONGAR

MAP REF: 89TL5403

Anglo-Saxon settlements in Essex can be traced to the 5th century and, by the 7th century, Christianity was established. St Andrew's at Greensted-juxta-Ongar was built in about AD850 and is the only surviving Saxon timber church in the world. Building was simple. A large oak beam was laid on the ground and joined to another, at roof height, by vertical oak trees split into two, their cut faces turned inwards like a stockade. The roof was thatched and there were no windows; light came from torches.

St Andrew's is an architectural student's dream – additions have been made in almost every century. Essential conservation work was carried out in the 19th century, replacing the rotted base timbers with a brick plinth.

▲ The *Cutty Sark*, queen of the 19th-century tea clippers, now rests in dry dock at Greenwich

Greensted is now just a suburb of Ongar, yet this rather ordinary little building is an important link in a venerable tradition, a symbol of a growing faith that would lead ultimately to the glories of Chartres and Durham.

GREENWICH

MAP REF: 88TQ3877

Greenwich was long ago absorbed into south-east London, but nothing can deprive it of its maritime history, its industrial heritage and its famous park. From its beginnings as a fishing village it has rarely been out of the mainstream of history, noticeably when the young Richard II negotiated, unsuccessfully, with Wat Tyler, and when George I stepped ashore to establish the Hanoverian succession.

Greenwich Park was first enclosed *c.*1428, as the park for the palace in which Henry VIII, Mary I and Elizabeth I would all be born. At the top is the Ranger's House, now a museum, with a number of splendid Jacobean and Stuart portraits. One of the best views of London has long been from the Park, near the Old Royal Observatory, also now a museum. Below the hill lie the buildings at the heart of Greenwich, the National Maritime Museum, the Queen's House and the Royal Naval College, and, beyond, the skyline of the capital.

The Maritime Museum has been greatly extended in recent years. Once a rather charmingly amateurish collection, it now incorporates the most modern museum advances. As for Greenwich Hospital, now the Royal Naval College, in addition to being partly designed by Wren, Hawksmoor and Vanbrugh, it has the Painted Hall by Thornhill, rivalling all but the best European work.

In dry dock near the entrance of the foot tunnel to the Isle of Dogs stand two reminders of past maritime glories – the magnificent 19th-century clipper, the *Cutty Sark*, and Sir Francis Chichester's *Gypsy Moth IV*, the tiny yacht in which he circumnavigated the world.

St Andrew's at Greensted, famous as the only surviving Saxon timber church ▼

Bordering Greenwich Park is historic **Blackheath**. Here, Tyler and Jack Cade led rebellions, and the people of London greeted Henry V after Agincourt and Charles II at the Restoration. Highwaymen frequented it, and the first games of golf in England were played over it. Today, Blackheath is a small open space, criss-crossed by roads, its character destroyed by years of building encroachments.

GUILDFORD

MAP REF: 91SU9949

William Cobbett, a Farnham man, thought Guildford 'the most agreeable' town he ever saw. The centre of the town is the High Street, full of fine buildings, and with views of the green slopes of Guildown beyond. Near the top, the Grammar School, founded in 1509, makes a fine start to a walk. The redbrick Abbot's Hospital is very striking and behind it a group of Jacobean almshouses form a lovely quadrangle. The very attractive 17th-century Guildford House is now an art gallery. Beyond is the guildhall, a remarkable mixture of styles with the famous town clock projecting over the street.

In a public park east of St Mary's Church is the keep, all that remains of the 12th-century castle. From it there is a view down to the River Wey. This most self-effacing of rivers slips through the town almost unnoticed, although providing a charming frame for the Yvonne Arnaud Theatre on its island site.

The See of Guildford was created in 1927 and the cathedral, designed by Sir Edward Maufe, was built between 1936 and 1961. Whatever may be thought of the brick exterior – it has been likened to an aircraft hangar – dramatically sited on Stag Hill, it is wonderfully light and airy inside. Close to the cathedral are the buildings of the University of Surrey which moved here from Battersea in 1966, bringing a fresh vigour to the town.

Guildford High Street's landmark ▼

▲ A cottage garden in Hambleden – a pretty Buckinghamshire village of brick-and-flint buildings

HADDENHAM

MAP REF: 86SP7308

Haddenham is now surrounded by modern developments, but the centre remains almost unspoilt with a network of streets, lanes and alleys best explored on foot. There are timber-framed houses – look for the thatched Church Farm by St Mary's Church – and many charming cottages. The Bone House is, rather eccentrically, decorated with the knuckle bones of sheep. Eccentricity is something of a tradition here, for how else can a village be described that possesses a High Street ending in a cul-de-sac!

Many of Haddenham's cottages and boundary walls were built of wichert – local chalk and clay, mixed with chopped straw and bound by water. The resultant cob was layered and given a rendering of plaster or rough-cast. Set on a base of stone, the walls and cottages were roofed by thatch or, more commonly, red pantiles. The almost continental effect is heightened by the Italian appearance of the large bell-tower of the church. The use of wichert, restricted to villages around Aylesbury, can also be seen at Dinton, Cuddington and Lower Winchendon.

HAMBLEDEN

MAP REF: 86SU7886

A picturesque village of two distinct parts, Hambleden has a charming centre, and, about a mile away, by the Thames, a secondary area with, as its centrepiece, one of Britain's most attractive mill buildings. Beautifully maintained, the white weatherboarded Hambleden Mill last milled corn in the 1950s and has been converted into flats, but can be studied from the nearby weir across the river. The first 'Varsity Boat Race took place between Hambleden Lock and Henley Bridge.

The main part of the village lies in a valley between beech-clad hills, with a stream running between predominately brick and flint cottages. The impression is of an estate village and so, in part, it is, for many of the cottages were built by the bookseller W H Smith. Caricatured as Sir Joseph Porter, 'Ruler of the Queen's Navee' in *H M S Pinafore*, when made 1st Lord of the Admiralty, Smith became the 1st Lord Hambleden, lived at Greenlands – now the Administrative Staff College – and is buried in Hambleden churchyard.

For a village of its size, Hambleden has some remarkable connections. In addition to W H Smith, St Thomas of Cantelupe, Bishop of Hereford and last English saint before the Reformation, was born on the site where the house known as Kenricks now stands. The Manor House was the birthplace of the 7th Earl of Cardigan, who led the Charge of the Light Brigade.

◄ Hampton Court's Privy Garden

HAMPSTEAD
MAP REF: 88TQ2685

A great part of London is composed of villages, and Hampstead is one of the most notable survivals as it has somehow retained its rural charm despite being engulfed by the capital. It was to **Hampstead Heath** that many of London's population fled at the time of the Great Fire and here the Government erected tents and organised disaster relief. Over succeeding centuries, the heath gained a reputation as a haunt of robbers, footpads and highwaymen, preying on travellers in and out of the City.

The 18th century saw the growth of mansions built by rich people anxious to live away from the centre of London and Kenwood is an example. It houses the Earl of Iveagh's Bequest of paintings by Rembrandt, Hals, Vermeer, Reynolds, Gainsborough and Turner, and a series of popular concerts is held by the lake each summer.

Glancing from the upper windows of Fenton House, a small William and Mary house with a magical

Bank holiday fun on Hampstead Heath ▼

walled garden, it is still possible to imagine the rural Hampstead of 200 years ago. The house contains furniture, superb porcelain and the important Benton Fletcher collection of early keyboard instruments.

Keats House is where the poet lived, next door to his fiancée, Fanny Brawne. It is now a museum of his life with letters, manuscripts and personal mementoes.

More recently, when Sigmund Freud escaped from occupied Vienna, he was able to bring many possessions with him, including the famous couch, other furniture and his library. All can be seen in his former home, now the Freud Museum.

HAMPTON COURT PALACE
MAP REF: 91TQ1568

Approaching the height of his powers in 1514, Cardinal Wolsey began building Hampton as his country home, but it soon developed into a great mansion, with more modern conveniences than any royal palace. Fifteen years later, after Wolsey had fallen out with Henry VIII, it was given to

the king – the gesture gained him nothing, and within months Wolsey was stripped of his remaining properties. Used first as a hunting lodge, Hampton became one of the king's favourite palaces and five of his six wives lived here.

The great gatehouse is a magnificent example of Tudor architecture as is the great hall, which replaced the original built by Wolsey. Henry was also responsible for the superb fan-vaulted timber roof in the chapel. In a very different style are the state apartments designed by Wren for William and Mary. Looked at from Fountain Court – now restored following a fire in 1985 – they resemble a French château.

George II was the last monarch to live at Hampton and a hundred years later it began to be opened to the public. The formal gardens, including delightful re-creations of the Tudor gardens, are a joy, as is the park, with its walks along the Thames. The maze, Henry's remarkable astronomical clock, the orangery, the Hampton Court Vine – its stem now measuring more than 7ft in circumference – all add to the fascination of this, one of London's most consistently popular historic houses.

HARLOW
MAP REF: 89TL4611

One of the towns developed from the New Towns Act of 1946, designed to ease congestion in major cities, Harlow was begun in 1947, and now houses 80,000 people. The residential area is divided into four, in green-field settings, and all within reach of the industrial areas of the town. The town centre is traffic free, the perimeter well supplied with car parks. As a way of improving the surroundings, sculptures have been commissioned and sited throughout the town.

Harlow Museum contains exhibits from the excavation of Harlow Roman Temple, a reminder to visitors that the town has a long history. In contrast, the Mark Hall Bicycle Museum deals with a 19th-century development, the bicycle, although the earliest exhibit is a Hobby Horse of 1818. Both these museums are housed in attractive settings – the town museum in a Georgian house with gardens and part of a moat from an earlier house, while the bicycle museum possesses three walled gardens, and a cottage and Tudor garden.

HATCHLANDS

MAP REF: 91TQ0652

Admiral Edward Boscawen, 'Old Dreadnought', moved to Hatchlands in 1749, replacing the existing building with a new, redbrick house, seven years later. Almost certainly he and his wife were, at least partially, their own architects, which may account for the fact that there are three sets of windows on the west side of the house, but only two on the south. Money acquired during the Admiral's French campaigns paid for the house, and the fine interior work by a young Robert Adam. This was an inspirational choice by the Boscawens, for Adam had only just returned from the Grand Tour and was an unknown.

Owned by the National Trust, Hatchlands contains a fine collection of keyboard instruments, including a pianoforte made for Marie Antoinette, lent by Alec Cobbe, the present tenant. The gardens are being restored and visitors now use the main entrance after years of entering through an Edwardian porch at the other end of the house (see page 75).

HATFIELD

MAP REF: 88TL2308

Hatfield is divided into two by the railway, now nearly 150 years old. Old Hatfield grew up around the palace of the Abbots and Bishops of Ely and lies to the east, with the New Town, largely developed in the 1930s and after World War II, to the west.

The most celebrated building in Hatfield is undoubtedly the handsome Jacobean Hatfield House, on the site of the Old Palace. The palace became Crown property in 1538 and was used by Henry VIII as a nursery for his children. Elizabeth I was kept under restraint at Hatfield by her sister Mary, and it was in the park that she learnt of her accession to the throne.

In 1608, Robert Cecil, 1st Earl of Salisbury, and Chief Minister to James I, agreed with the king to exchange his great house, Theobalds, for the Old Palace. The bulk he knocked down, retaining only the western range containing the banqueting hall, as a separate building – today it is used for Elizabethan banquets. Cecil died in 1612, the year Hatfield was finished, but his descendants still live here in what is, by common consent, one of the finest houses in the country.

The death of the Dowager Lady Salisbury in a fire which destroyed much of the west wing of the house in 1835 was covered by a young reporter, Charles Dickens, who later used Hatfield in *Oliver*

Bluebell time at Hatchlands. The garden was designed by Humphry Repton and Gertrude Jekyll ▼

Twist and some short stories.

The Old Mill House Museum and Mill at Mill Green, run by the local council, closes only on Christmas Day, and the large working water wheel, restored in the 1980s, is used to produce freshly ground flour. The museum houses archaeological finds from the Hatfield area while some of the cottages are believed to be among the oldest in Hertfordshire.

▲ Hornbeams in Hatfield Forest

HATFIELD FOREST

MAP REF: 88TL5521

Owned and sympathetically managed for two centuries by the Houblon family, Hatfield is the nearest we now have to a medieval Royal Forest. The long rides and open chases survive, as does the hornbeam, the most significant tree of ancient forests, with the oak. At Hatfield good examples of both can be seen in the 12 coppice areas, looking much as they did before destruction and bad forestry practice endangered most of the great forests (see Epping page 42). Since 1924 the Forest has been owned by the National Trust which is implementing a plan, including restoring coppicing and cutting the older pollards, intended to return the Forest, at least partially, to working order. Cattle, deer and a rabbit warren, scrub, fen and grassland all play their part in preserving this unique survival of the Middle Ages.

There is a pleasant, tree-fringed lake, made in the 18th century, and now incorporated into a Site of Special Scientific Interest. Details of fishing and boat hire are available in the Shell House overlooking the lake. Originally a grotto, this has flint, shells and glass fragments in its highly decorated walls, with displays explaining how coppicing, pollarding and grazing are being organised.

HAXTED WATERMILL

MAP REF: 93TQ4246

This restored 16th-century water mill lies on the B2028 between Lingield and Edenbridge on Eden Water.

Apart from the working machinery of the mill, including two waterwheels, there is a display of agricultrual implements. Another attraction is the picture gallery on one floor of the mill where hundreds of photographs of mills from all over the country can be seen.

An illustrated display of the local entries for the Domesday survey is another feature, and last but not least there is a Children's Surprise.

HEMEL HEMPSTEAD

MAP REF: 87TL0507

Unlike several of the other 'new towns' built since the late 1940s, Hemel Hempstead has a long history. Set on a hill along the River Gade, it was an attractive market town and fortunate in that the development of the new town had little effect on the old. The High Street is still very pleasant, with medieval timber-framed houses and Georgian brick buildings, some retaining bow-fronted windows.

St Mary's is the largest Norman church in the county, dating from 1150, and possesses more of architectural merit than St Alban's. The chancel has a rib-vaulted roof (the only one in the county) and the nave is supremely Norman with a contemporary clerestory above. Outside, the central tower has a leaded wooden spire, 200ft high. This elegant 14th-century addition is the best of the very few wooden spires of the period to survive – Chesterfield is perhaps better known because of its twist.

Until the 19th century, **Bovingdon** and **Flaunden** were part of the parish of Hemel Hempstead. Both have some medieval houses and cottages, and Bovingdon's 19th-century church has a marvellous medieval effigy of a knight in armour. Flaunden had a chapel of similar age in a remote spot by the River Chess, but it was allowed to fall into ruin with squatters occupying it during the last century.

HENLEY-ON-THAMES

MAP REF: 86SU7682

Superbly sited on the River Thames, the market town of

Henley has more than 300 listed buildings. One of the oldest is the 14th-century, timber-framed Chantry House, its upper floor consisting of a large, aisled room, divided into bays. An important stop on the London to Oxford coach route, Henley retains many fine inns; some of these, and many other buildings, now have Georgian frontages. The Kenton Theatre, approaching its second century, is one of Britain's oldest. The fine five-arched bridge replaced an earlier one in 1786. With the Angel Hotel and the parish church, it forms the main elements of a much-photographed view from Remenham Hill on the London side of the town.

The long-established brewing family of Brakspear have their brewery in Henley – they must be the only brewers with papal connections, Nicholas Brakspear having been Pope in the 12th century. Some beer, but more champagne, is consumed each summer during the internationally renowned Royal Regatta held here on one of the few straight stretches of the Thames.

Fawley Court (Marian Fathers Historic House and Museum) lies close to Henley Reach, on the Marlow road. Built in 1684 as a family residence, the house has an unsurpassed pedigree – designed by Wren and remodelled by James Wyatt, decorated by Grinling Gibbons, set in a park by Capability Brown! The famous temple on Temple Island, where the regatta starts, was designed by

Wyatt. The museum contains a library with a range of memorabilia relating to Polish culture, kings and army.

A few miles west of Henley is the manor house of **Greys Court**. The present, Elizabethan, house incorporates parts of a 12th-century fortified house but is one of the most charming, and least war-like of houses, partly because of the mellowness of its brick and flint surface. Visitors can see the well-house, complete with vast donkey-wheel (but no donkey!), and try the unique maze, with its religious theme, completed only in 1981.

SMART SPORT

Two of the smartest sporting events in the calendar are staged in the summer: the Royal Ascot race meeting and the Henley Royal Regatta. Both are part of the old London 'season', the round of social events which fashionable people liked to see

and be seen at, and both still have considerable cachet.

The racecourse on Ascot Heath was laid out in 1711 on the instructions of Queen Anne. It is not far from Windsor Castle and royalty has always taken a keen interest in it. At the Royal Ascot meeting in June the Queen and other members of the royal

A rowing eight, complete with cox and lucky mascot, at Henley ▼

Hertford Castle's gatehouse, set in lovely gardens, now provides a home for the council's offices ▶

▲ The riverside at Henley where motor launches of all kinds, rowing boats, skiffs and canoes can be hired

HERTFORD
MAP REF: 88TL3212

The county town, Hertford developed from two Saxon forts built near the ford across the River Lea. It lacks outstanding buildings but those in Fore Street are nicely varied and include the 18th-century shire hall and a Tudor courtyard inn, the Salisbury Arms. Parliament Square is so named because Parliament met three times in the castle during the 16th century to escape the Plague. The

family drive along the course in open carriages to the loyal approval of gentlemen in top hats and morning dress, and ladies in amazing hats. The principal race is the Gold Cup, run since 1807 over two-and-a-half miles, England's premier long-distance flat race.

The regatta at Henley-on-Thames in the first week of July goes back to 1839 and became 'royal' in 1851, when the Prince Consort was Patron. Besides attracting past and present rowing men in finery of blazers and coloured caps to picnic on cold salmon and champagne, it is the most prestigious rowing meeting in the world. The Grand Challenge Cup, contested ever since 1839, attracts the best rowing eights on the globe and the Diamond Challenge Sculls, rowed since 1884, is considered the single oarsman's 'blue riband'.

Quaker Meeting House, behind a walled courtyard, is the oldest in the world in continual use for worship. Separated from the rest of the old town by a dual carriageway, West Street has a number of houses built between the 17th and 19th centuries.

The castle was probably built on the site of one of the Saxon burghs. Since 1906 the 15th-century gatehouse, all that remains, has been used as administrative offices by the council. The grounds, containing traces of the castle, are a public park.

HEVER CASTLE
MAP REF: 93TQ4846

Hever is a tiny, 13th-century semi-fortified manor house – it was never a castle – with a double moat, beside a 'Tudor' village. Both the inside of the castle and the village are brilliant re-creations and, in the case of the village, one of the most original solutions to the problem of space ever devised. When the American branch of the Astor family bought Hever in 1903 they found the house too cramped and so William Waldorf Astor and his architect built a medieval village connected to the castle by a covered bridge. This 'village' actually contained guest rooms, offices, servants' quarters and

kitchens – ideal for its latest use as a conference centre!

Visitors are able to enjoy the period furniture in the castle and the elaborate Italianate gardens. Like so much else, the gardens are less than 100 years old, having been designed for Astor. By contrast, some of their statuary and sculpture dates back 2,000 years. One thousand workmen spent four years creating the garden and the lake, made by diverting the River Eden.

Anne Boleyn lived here until she married Henry VIII in 1533 and it is, somehow, typical of Henry that, after the death of her parents, he should take possession of Hever and pass it to Anne of Cleves following their marriage and divorce in 1540, four years after Anne Boleyn had died on Tower Green!

Hever Castle, onetime home to Anne Boleyn, now a conference centre ▼

HIGH WYCOMBE
MAP REF: 86SU8693

In the Victorian period certain country towns became associated with a specific industry. At High Wycombe, as lace making died out, so the manufacture of chairs developed from a semi-rural craft to one of national importance. Not surprisingly the town's museum, the Wycombe Local History and Chair Museum, near the station, features objects illustrating the furniture industry, with an emphasis on the 'Windsor' chair, supported by displays on pillow lace and other local craft industries.

The guildhall of 1757 sometimes holds exhibitions but must be seen for its own sake – it is a most attractive building. Though the market hall, opposite, is by Robert Adam, it is less pleasing, suffering from a dome roof added at the beginning of this century. Both these rather grand buildings were the gift of the local Shelburne family. The Earl of Shelburne, later 1st Marquess of Lansdowne, is one of five Prime Ministers buried in Buckinghamshire; he lies, without monument, in the family vault in All Saints' Church.

With few exceptions, the rest of the centre of High Wycombe has disappeared under a sea of concrete. The Rye is an ancient common which has survived, with a tollhouse to the south of the London road.

The guildhall in High Wycombe ▼

BODGERS AT WORK

The chair-making industry flourished in the Chiltern beechwoods in the 18th and 19th centuries, with High Wycombe as its principal centre. Some of the work was carried on in the heart of the woods by the 'bodgers', as they were called – the name had no connotation of poor workmanship. Bodgers spent most of their lives moving through the woods, living in rickety shacks which they assembled at each stopping point. They looked for suitable timber for chair legs and struts, which they turned on primitive pole-lathes and sent in to workshops in High Wycombe or Penn or Stokenchurch, where the main pieces of the chairs were made and all the parts were assembled.

The bodgers were chair leg specialists, but they also made stools, tent pegs and spokes for wheels. Moving from one

▲ High Wycombe's museum

clearing to another, they lived in balance with Nature. They took only the wood that was of use to them and by letting a bit of light and space in they encouraged the growth of straight saplings, and so put back as much as they used up.

Bodging was still going full tilt between the two world wars and even as late as 1950 a few elderly craftsmen were still practising their traditional occupation.

HINDHEAD
MAP REF: 90SU8835

Cobbett called Hindhead 'the most villainous spot that God ever made', but that was before it became very popular as a place to live in or to retire to in the late 19th century. Hindhead now has many large houses, the majority built at that time, carefully protected from prying eyes by banks of rhododendrons, while pine trees soften the edge of the greensand ridge.

In addition to being the second highest part of Surrey at 894ft, Hindhead possesses two major natural features. The Devil's Punch Bowl is a hollow of dry, sandy heath, sloping steeply to a wetter habitat at the bottom where the Smallbrook stream flows. There are waymarked walks, but the whole area is suffering from erosion. The A3 curves round the Punch Bowl, with the old coach road to Portsmouth hidden in trees on the left. Above the road is Gibbet Hill, so named because three men were hanged here for the murder of a sailor walking to Portsmouth. From the open area at the summit there are immense views south and east into Kent, Surrey, Sussex and Hampshire, while the view from the Punch Bowl includes the Chilterns.

Both these areas form part of Hindhead Commons, purchased for the National Trust in the early years of this century by local people worried over the rapid spread of houses. The total owned by the Trust is now 1,400 acres.

HODDESDON
MAP REF: 88TL3708

Though a comparatively late development, Hoddesdon was a market town by the 13th century. It lies, next to the manor of Broxbourne, which it served, on the Saxon road along the Lea

▲ Furnace Pond, near Horsmonden, was a source of power

valley, east of Roman Ermine Street. Pilgrims on their way to the shrine at Walsingham worshipped in a 14th-century chapel which was replaced in 1732. Incorporated into the new parish church of 1864–5, the chapel adds a touch of elegance to the interior.

The brick-built, Victorian clock-tower stands at the centre of the town. Hogges Hall, Rawdon House and Lowewood House are worth noting in the High Street, as is the Lloyd's Bank building. Here the great road engineer John McAdam lived with his second wife, whom he married at the age of 71, to the disapproval of his family. Lowewood House is now a museum. In the garden there is a statue known as 'The Samaritan Woman' which stood in the market place for nearly 200 years from 1631 as the conduit head for the supply of fresh water to the town.

See separate entry for Rye House, page 64:

HORSMONDEN
MAP REF: 93TQ7040

There is a replica of a 17th-century gun at the Gun Inn at Horsmonden – a reminder that gun-making was a speciality of the Wealden iron industry which flourished here during the Middle Ages. **Furnace Pond**, a large hammer pond some half-mile from the village, provided water power to drive the hammers to beat the iron into shape. Both Charles I and Oliver Cromwell owned Horsmonden guns, while the original of the inn's gun is now in the Tower of London.

The 14th-century sandstone Church of St Margaret is one-and-a-half miles from the present village and, as elsewhere, a number of explanations have been advanced for this, but the possibility of plague, followed by re-siting in a healthier area, is the most likely. Closer to the village, Sprivers is an 18th-century house in a lovely garden. Owned by the National Trust, it is tenanted. Garden ornaments are sold here and the garden is open once a week.

An enchanting Wealden hillside village on a back road to Goudhurst, **Brenchley**, like Horsmonden, was once a centre of the iron industry – 200 men from the village were employed in the industry at its peak. As a result, the quality of much of the building is high, with white weatherboarded houses and Tudor cottages. The half-timbered house behind the

war memorial is one of five 16th-century houses of this type within a mile of the centre of the village.

Matfield has a very attractive grouping of houses behind the village pond with, at its centre, a fine Georgian manor house. The writer Siegfried Sassoon lived in Matfield and there is a plaque on his house on the road to Paddock Wood. A short distance out of the village is the 17th-century **Crittenden Manor**. It has a delightful garden, sometimes open, where good use has been made of two furnace ponds.

HUGHENDEN MANOR
MAP REF: 86SU8695

Hughenden was Benjamin Disraeli's home for the last 33 years of his life. Here he returned to relax with his beloved Mary Anne, and here his political strategy was planned. A plain white stuccoed house, about 100 years old when Disraeli bought it in 1847, it was converted into a typically High Victorian home, faced in redbrick, and decorated with a few Gothic pinnacles. The Gothic theme is continued, with greater success, inside, where the National Trust maintain several rooms as they were when Disraeli lived here. The library reflects his passion for books, and the study is very evocative with black-edged notepaper, always used after his wife's death, still on the writing table. Hughenden is remarkable, not for what it is, a rather pleasing family home, but because of what it reveals of the man behind the complex, radical, politician who lived here.

Queen Victoria accorded only two of her Prime Ministers – Melbourne and Disraeli – the honour of a visit to their home. At Disraeli's death, her wreath was of primroses, 'his favourite flower from Osborne'. Disraeli and Mary Anne are buried together in the churchyard of the Church of St Michael, set a little below the

house. Around church and house stand the trees that he planted and, in spring, the primroses he loved so much.

IGHTHAM MOTE
MAP REF: 93TQ5956

Ightham is one of the most romantic houses in a county which has more than its fair share of such buildings. Predominantly 14th-century, but with a mix of styles that harmonise remarkably well, it lies deep in a hidden valley, surrounded by trees. The first sighting is breathtaking, a small manor house, part Kentish stone, part timber-framed, rising sheer from a moat. Once through the courtyard and inside the visitor is immediately at the heart of the house – the great hall, one of the finest in existence. But the house has much more to offer, including the rib-vaulted crypt, supporting the original chapel. It, and the solar, were converted into living rooms when the Tudor chapel was added. This has wonderful panelling and a marvellous roof decorated with painted motifs of the Tudor and Aragon families. Beyond, and a total contrast, is the spacious drawing room, with a fireplace carved with the arms of the Selbys who owned Ightham for three centuries.

An American, Charles Henry Robinson, fell in love with Ightham in his youth and bought it many years later. There is now a simple tablet in the wall of the crypt and behind it lie the ashes of Mr Robinson. The house he loved has passed, as he wished, to the National Trust, which is carefully restoring it.

Ightham village is two miles away and tends to be ignored by visitors hurrying to the Mote – a pity, for the village has some good buildings, including the George & Dragon pub, while the church is interesting, not least since it contains memorials to *two* holders of the Victoria Cross. South of the Mote are **Plaxtol** and **Old Soar Manor** (see page 77).

INGATESTONE
MAP REF: 89TQ6499

Ingatestone has a pleasing mixture of architectural styles from several centuries on show in its main street. The church has a splendid tower of redbrick with patterns in black, and a chapel containing the tombs of the Petre family. The tower is older than Ingatestone Hall, their home, built by Sir William Petre around the 1550s. In the 18th century the west wing was demolished and the rest divided into flats; only in this century has the family returned, restoring the house. Today, Essex County Council lease and open the north wing and long gallery which includes a portrait of Arabella Fermor. The 7th Lord Petre stole a lock of her hair, starting a rather silly family feud which was only resolved following publication of Pope's 'Rape of the Lock'.

Among the villages lying close to the A12, and in the vicinity of Ingatestone, are **Mountnessing** and **Stock**. Both have tower windmills, owned by Essex County Council, that can be viewed by appointment. Mountnessing Mill is in full working order.

IVINGHOE
MAP REF: 86SP9416

Ivinghoe has some splendid houses, including a Tudor manor house and a fine Georgian building, now a youth hostel. The bench-ends in the Church of St Mary have a remarkable series of carvings depicting the long-haired 'green man' of medieval mythology. For those with an interest in industrial archaeology, Ford End Watermill is in the village, and Pitstone Windmill nearby. Ford End is a three-storey building with an overshot wheel and internal machinery. It last worked in the 1960s and slow progress is being made on restoring it. Pitstone is a restored smock mill, owned by the National Trust. Parts of the mill date back to the early 17th century.

The five-acre Iron Age hillfort on **Ivinghoe Beacon**, one mile to the east of the village, is another Trust property believed, like Pitstone Mill, to be the oldest of its kind in the country. It has a single bank and ditch, with a Bronze Age round barrow on the summit where the Ridgeway Path ends its 90-mile journey from Avebury in Wiltshire.

JORDANS
MAP REF: 86SU9791

Jordans is a secluded hill village with a peaceful green in an area long associated with the Quaker movement, although the village is a self-governing garden community built by Friends in the 1920s. The Meeting House is a touchingly simple building, erected in 1688 when the persecution of non-conformists was ended by James II's Declaration of Indulgence. The graveyard contains the bodies of William Penn, founder of Pennsylvania, his two wives and 10 of his children.

Old Jordans was a farmhouse owned by the Friends, and used by Penn and others for meetings until the Meeting House was built. Across the garden is the Mayflower Barn, almost certainly containing timbers from the little ship that carried the Pilgrim Fathers to America in 1620.

KENSWORTH
MAP REF: 87TL0319

The Church of St Mary has elements dating back to about 1120, but the most obvious external feature is the Victorian patterned roof – light tiles in diamond shapes on a grey background. Above the south door there is an interesting, but worn, carving on two surfaces, illustrating a fox under attack by a crane. The church is part of a quietly pretty group, standing among trees, with a well-maintained farm, outbuildings and cottages. They are on a steep rise away from the main village at Kensworth Common.

The houses on the Common are not exciting, although the old school is pleasant, but there is a third, more interesting, group of buildings along a lane to the east of the church, at **Kensworth Lynch**. The best is Lynch House, an attractive late 18th-century brick building, surrounded by half-timbered houses, probably 17th- and early 18th-century and all very smartly presented.

Kew's huge Palm House. The Royal Botanical Garden is primarily a research institution but its 300 acres are enjoyed by thousands each year ▶

KEW

MAP REF: 92TQ1876

It was George III's mother, Princess Augusta, who commissioned the development of botanical gardens at Kew. Work began in 1751 and the **Royal Botanic Garden** was opened to the public in 1841. Visually, the gardens are probably best known for the 163ft-high pagoda, erected in 1761 as one of a series of decorative buildings, but the many glasshouses are of more practical value. Decimus Burton's vast glass and wrought-iron Palm House is still probably the best known, although the most remarkable must be the Princess of Wales Conservatory, with its 10 different temperature zones allowing displays of plants from habitats as diverse as deserts and cloud forest. More than 50,000 different species of plants are cultivated at Kew, and it is still the world's foremost botanical research establishment.

Within the grounds is Kew Palace, the most homely of London's palaces – and hardly a 'real' palace at all. Originally

▲ Knebworth House – Gothic extravagance set in a park providing attractions for all ages and tastes

known as the Dutch House, it owes only superficial allegiance to that style, but it did become part of the royal estates at the end of the 18th century when a new palace was planned beside it, though never completed. George III and Queen Charlotte lived, briefly, in the Dutch House and the Queen used it as a dower house until her death in 1818. The garden, between house and river, is very prettily laid out in formal 17th-century style, although dating only from 1975.

At **Brentford**, next door, the Kew Bridge Steam Museum contains five Cornish beam pump engines, said to represent a quarter of the world's surviving examples. Three of them, and other steam engines, are run regularly.

The Musical Museum in the High Street has an incredible selection of automatic musical instruments, from Wurlitzers to a self-playing violin (see page 75).

KNEBWORTH

MAP REF: 88TL2520

From the outside, Knebworth House is a mind-bending mass of turrets, towers and battlements looking like an American film set of 'Merrie England'. Under this, much altered, is part of an earlier building – the west wing of a 15th-

century courtyard house. Originally a Tudor great hall, it was transformed into a banqueting hall in Jacobean times and further altered in the early 19th century by Mrs Elizabeth Bulwer, whose family has lived here for 500 years. She began the extension and Gothicising of the house, completed by her younger son, Sir Edward Bulwer-Lytton. Mrs Bulwer disapproved of his marriage, and cut him off. Forced to make a living, he wrote novels, at which he proved highly successful. Inheriting the house in 1843, he created one of the great examples of High Victorian architecture with, inside, an incredible pseudo-Jacobean staircase.

Many notable visitors have stayed at Knebworth, including Dickens, who brought his own company of amateur actors here in 1850. The gardens were designed by Lutyens and incorporate a herb garden by Gertrude Jekyll.

The Countryside Commission sponsors the country park, set in a 250-acre deer park and offering a range of attractions including horse-riding, a steam railway and a railway museum. Recently, Knebworth has become known for its major rock concerts.

▲ The central tower and gatehouse of Knole. This huge house, one of the largest in England, is surrounded by a lovely deer park

KNOLE
MAP REF: 93TQ5455

The approach to Knole is through a short, narrow lane leading from the main road in Sevenoaks. Almost at once the road enters the deer park, a total contrast to the busy town. Winding between tree- and bracken-clad hillocks, it offers brief glimpses of the house ahead. Suddenly, as the road sweeps up to the car park, where fallow deer invariably feed, the overwhelming size of Knole becomes apparent. The visitor is facing the long west front, formed by a series of Dutch gables spreading out from a central tower and gatehouse. Behind this appears a jumble of roofs, chimneys, turrets and courtyards, resembling a fortified village more than a house.

Yet the first house on the site was a medieval manor, purchased and made into a palace in the 15th century by Thomas Bourchier, Archbishop of Canterbury. Cranmer 'gave' Knole to Henry VIII and the king spent a fortune continuing its expansion.

Elizabeth I passed the house to Sir Thomas Sackville, who employed vast numbers of men, including specially imported Italians, to work on the internal furnishings, and to build no less than three long galleries! His descendants still live at Knole, which is now owned by the National Trust.

Containing a unique collection of 17th- and 18th-century furniture, and filled with silver and paintings – of which Horace Walpole said, 'bespoke by the yard, and drawn all by the same painter' – Knole is a positive riot of visual delight, needing several visits to fully appreciate it. The ostentatious grandeur and display of wealth reaches its peak in the King's room with the Louis XIV bed made for the marriage of James II.

Outside again, visitors can wander around 1,000 acres of parkland, returning slowly from past to present, for there is, inside Knole, a sensation of timelessness (see page 77).

LAMBERHURST
MAP REF: 93TQ6736

The attractiveness of Lamberhurst is sometimes overlooked, since it lies across the A21 and suffers from a major traffic problem – a long-promised bypass has failed to materialise. The village lies in a valley, with the best houses climbing the hill on the London side. Typically Wealden, they are tile-hung and weatherboarded, with one fine timber-framed house, Coggers Hall. Lamberhurst is particularly fortunate in its pubs which are attractive buildings with genuine atmosphere.

One of the most successful mixes of the genuine and the artificial can be found at Scotney Castle, south of the village. The little ruined castle – a combination of 14th-century fortification and 17th-century manor – stands on an island surrounded by a moat created by damming the River Bewl. In the 19th century the owners, the Hussey family, decided to build a new house on the hill overlooking the castle and to fashion a picturesque garden. Stone for the house, a Jacobean pastiche, was quarried from the hill, opening the view to the castle and moat. The area was then planted with a wonderful variety of shrubs, trees and flowers.

At the Owl House, Maureen, Marchioness of Dufferin and Ava, created a lovely small garden around an equally charming timber-framed cottage. The contrast between this essentially 'homely' garden and Scotney is considerable, but they complement each other beautifully.

Just over the border into Sussex are the ruins, landscaped by Repton, of Bayham Abbey, a small Premonstratensian abbey built c.1200. Near by is Bartley Mill, originally the abbey mill, with a history reaching back to the 13th century. Refurbished, it now grinds flour for sale.

A typically English garden surrounds Owl House, a smuggler's cottage ▼

LIMPSFIELD
MAP REF: 92TQ4053

A narrow village street, full of pleasing vernacular buildings, is at the heart of Limpsfield.

To the south lie Limpsfield Chart and Common, owned by the Forestry Commission and the National Trust. It is an area of mixed woodland and heath, particularly popular in autumn when the beech trees provide magnificent colour. At Limpsfield Chart a colony of Simple Life intellectuals attempted, around the end of the last century, to perpetuate a rural life-style already fast disappearing. They published books and tracts, but the realities of smallholding defeated them, as they did many similar groups in the years between the two World Wars.

LOSELEY HOUSE
MAP REF: 90SU9747

Just over two miles south-west of Guildford is Elizabethan Loseley House. The name may be familiar to many because of the dairy products, ice-cream, yogurt, etc, from the estate farm which offers tours, walks and trailer rides as an outdoor alternative to the house (see page 76).

LULLINGSTONE
MAP REF: 93TQ5265

Lullingstone Castle has belonged to the Hart Dyke family for 600 years. The house (it was never a castle) is, largely, a Queen Anne house – quite literally so, as the Queen stayed here and the shallow

treads on the stairs and the bath house, near by, were both for her benefit. The Parish Church of St Botolph within the walls of the castle is full of grand monuments to the family and some of the glass, like the church, is 14th-century. For many years the Lullingstone Silk Farm was sited here and provided silk for royalty. Although now in Dorset, the farm retains its original name. Lullingstone Park, once the park of the castle, consists of 300 acres of natural oak and beechwood. It overlooks the Darent valley above **Shoreham**, the centre of which remains as pleasing as when Samuel Palmer lived here and

painted his beloved *Valley of Vision*.

A walk through the park leads to **Lullingstone Roman Villa**, built within 30 or 40 years of the Roman conquest of Britain and burnt down in the 5th century. It was rediscovered in the 18th century but not excavated until after World War II. Among the features in this magnificent villa are a particularly fine mosaic floor of about AD380, depicting Europa and the Bull, another of Bellerophon, mounted on Pegasus, killing the Chimaera, and a unique Christian chapel, making Lullingstone one of the earliest Christian sites in Britain. The history of Lullingstone Roman Villa is well documented and the outline of the various rooms clearly traceable (see page 75).

LUTON HOO
MAP REF: 87TL1018

Luton Hoo is an attractive house remodelled, in Palladian style, by Robert Adam around an older building. It was added to twice in the 19th century, with a final flourish in 1903. Luton Hoo is set in a fine 1,500-acre park, with two lakes, landscaped by Capability Brown at a cost of £10,000. Yet, for the majority of visitors, these are just adjuncts to the purpose of a visit to the house.

Inside, the house is furnished in the height of Edwardian fashion, with rooms brilliantly decorated in white and gold, and paintings, tapestries, furniture, jewels, and porcelain, topped by a collection of Fabergé pieces few national collections can equal. All this was brought together by Sir Julius Wernher, who had made a fortune as a diamond magnate in South Africa. To supplement this

Luton Hoo, which houses a fabulous collection of Fabergé porcelain ▼

richness, the late Lady Zia Wernher, grand-daughter of Czar Nicholas I and daughter-in-law of Sir Julius, added a remarkable collection of portraits and mementoes of the Czars.

Less than a mile from Luton Hoo are the remains of **Someries Castle**. Once an important fortified manor, it passed through many hands before being acquired in the early 1700s by the Napier family who preferred Luton Hoo and partially dismantled Someries. Today only the ruins of the gatehouse and chapel survive, but they have the distinction of being the oldest buildings in the county to be built almost entirely of brick.

MAIDENHEAD
MAP REF: 90SU8980

The river-crossing at Maidenhead was important from medieval times and when the attractive road bridge across the Thames was built in 1772 the town was already a staging post on the London-to-Bath road (the A4). Later, the arrival of the railway ensured the town's continued prosperity. The great railway bridge by Brunel features in Turner's *Rain, Steam and Speed*, painted in 1844, six years after the bridge was completed.

Today, Maidenhead is a popular commuter town with many exceptionally 'des. res.' on its extensive river frontage. London is only a short journey away by car or train, and modern commuters are continuing a trend set by the Edwardians. The town still has a few coaching inns and a group of 17th-century almshouses, but the centre is best described as functional.

Near by is the **Courage Shire Horse Centre** where horses, harness and brasses can be seen. There are guided tours, a tea room and a shop here as well.

MARLOW

MAP REF: 90SU8486

The period around 1800 provides many of the attractive houses in Marlow, although the oldest building is the Old Parsonage, parts of which date back to the 14th century. Dick Turpin is said to have drunk in the Crown, in the High Street, and a milestone in front of it comes from the turnpike route built by the Cecils of Hatfield (see page 51) between their house and the Bath road at Reading. West Street has several literary connections; Thomas Love Peacock lived at No 47 and the Shelleys at No 104. In this unlikely setting Mary wrote *Frankenstein*. However, the Two Brewers seems wholly appropriate for Jerome K Jerome while sketching out parts of *Three Men in a Boat*!

The suspension bridge over the Thames was built in the same year, 1832, as the parish church, although the monuments inside All Saints' are older. The most interesting depicts the death of one Sir Miles Hobart in a coaching accident in London.

MEOPHAM

MAP REF: 93TQ6466

Meopham's large, triangular green has a cricket pitch, a pavilion, a celebrated pub and a splendid smock mill, built early last century. The mill is unusual in that it is hexagonal, not octagonal. The ground floor is used as a parish room while the upper floors are presented as they would have appeared when the mill was operating.

A few miles to the west through lovely downland is the tiny village of **Ash**, with its charming group of church, rectory and Charles II house. In recent years it has been somewhat overshadowed by its modern cousin, the ultimate 1960s village of **New Ash Green**. An interesting, ambitious concept comprising small hamlets in a mixture of styles and materials, linked by wooded areas and pathways, the project failed to catch the public imagination and was never completed.

South of Meopham is **Trottiscliffe** – locally pronounced Trosley and now widely accepted as such – where the artist Graham Sutherland lived for some years, by the green, in the weatherboarded White House. The church has a remarkable pulpit originally made for Westminster Abbey. In the 19th century the owners of the Trosley Towers estate planted many flowering shrubs which form the basis of the underplanting of the fine trees now established in the **Trosley Country Park**. Many walks and nature trails have been laid out in this mixture of wood, scrub and open chalk, where a number of orchid species grow among the many wild flowers. One trail leads to the **Coldrum Stones**, a small, well-preserved Neolithic long barrow similar to that at **Kit's Coty** some miles away across the Medway valley.

MUCH HADHAM

MAP REF: 89TL4219

A large village, often referred to as the prettiest in the county, Much Hadham has a positive catalogue of handsome houses. Yew Tree House and Woodham House are 17th-century, The Lordship, North Leys and Much Hadham Hall are Georgian, while the White House is 19th-century Gothic. Interspersed with all this are humble, timber-framed and weatherboarded cottages, some dating to Elizabethan times. Moor Place stands in its own park – a beautiful house by an almost unknown Scottish architect, Robert Mitchell.

Next to the Church of St Andrew stands what was, for 800 years, the country palace of the Bishops of London and birthplace of Edmund Tudor, father of Henry VII. The presence of the palace enhanced the prosperity of the village which in 1851 boasted over 50 tradesmen and shopkeepers, and 11 professional people in 250 households. Inside the church there is a 13th-century oak door, but of particular interest are the king and queen headstops beside the west door. They are the gift of Henry Moore, who lived at nearby Perry Green from 1941 until his death in 1986.

PENN

MAP REF: 86SU9193

The Penn family took their name from this ridge-top Chiltern village with its magnificent views south to Hindhead (see page 54) 50 miles away. The tranquil village green is surrounded by 17th-century cottages while there are some fine white-painted houses along the ridge. Inside Holy Trinity Church there is a Norman font, a 12th-century stone coffin, many brass memorials and, the greatest treasure, a medieval Doom painting on oak boards. Probably hidden in the roof at the Reformation, it was not rediscovered until 1938, when it was recognised just as the panels were to be burnt as scrap!

William Penn, founder of Pennsylvania, was *not* part of this branch of the Penn family, although four of his grandsons are buried in Penn churchyard. His connections are with nearby Jordans (see page 56), where he and both his wives are buried.

Geographically part of Penn, **Tylers Green** is a separate parish, with its own pond overlooked by flint houses. To the north, Penn Street has a Victorian church beautifully set against Chiltern beeches.

◄ A 225ft suspension bridge spans the Thames at Marlow. There are particularly lovely views from here

▲ Penshurst Place, where the Elizabethan poet Philip Sidney was born. The walled gardens and parkland are rather less formal than the great house

PENSHURST

MAP REF: 93TQ5243

Penshurst village is superb, full of attractive buildings with a timeless air about it. Yet it is one of the classic examples of a 19th-century model village, expensively re-created using traditional methods and styles. The church, however, is basically 14th-century and the rectory, 18th-century. Combined with the almshouses and cottages – some genuinely old – they make Penshurst one of the most picturesque in a county that is blessed with many picture-book villages.

Penshurst Place, the large house above the valley where the rivers Eden and Medway meet, was built by Sir John de Pulteney, wool merchant and four times Lord Mayor of London, in the 1340s. Its main feature is the great hall, one of the first to escape from the style of a medieval aisled barn which had persisted since Norman times. It has a magnificent chestnut-timbered roof and, like Ightham (see page 55), it has tall windows, still owing much to church architecture. It is a vast room, 62ft long and almost the same in height at its apex. Nothing else in the house can match it, although Queen Elizabeth's room and the long gallery would each be a major feature in most houses.

Penshurst was granted by Edward VI to his steward, Sir William Sidney, in 1552. William's older son, Henry, added the two main wings to the house in which the Sidney family still live. His son, Philip, was born here in 1554 and is best remembered as a favourite of Elizabeth I and for his poetry.

There is a toy museum in the house, and a 10-acre walled garden, a park, a farm museum in a traditional barn, and several other attractions.

MONUMENTS AND MEMORIALS

'Avice returned to that dust from whence she sprang and . . . the unrelenting King of Terrors triumphed over Thomas.' Thus the grim inscription on the 16th-century tomb of Thomas and Avice Mildmay in Chelmsford Cathedral.

The Mildmays were the leading family in Chelmsford. Making their money in trade, they turned into country gentry. The prosperity of the area near London is reflected in a wealth of other monuments and memorials to the local families who once ran the countryside: from squires – the Halseys at Great Missenden, the Lyttons at Knebworth, the Hobys at Bisham – to great landed magnates like the Russells, Dukes of Bedford, who were interred generation by generation with monuments of fabulous grandeur in their exclusive separate chapel in the church at Chenies.

From medieval Crusaders in armour to obese 17th-century gentlemen in monstrous periwigs, Georgian mourning nymphs and sad Victorian essays on the pain of loss, the monuments contain a rich history of changing taste, fashion and attitudes. At Cobham in Kent, for instance, the Church of St Mary Magdalene is famous for its brasses to the lords of the manor from the 14th to the 16th centuries. The knights are in chain mail, helmeted, with sword and dagger on hip, hands clasped in prayer – the image of the Christian warrior. Placed with majestic arrogance in the middle of the chancel is a monument of an entirely different stamp, the tomb chest of an Elizabethan Lord Cobham. He and his wife recline side by side in effigy and below, round the sides, their children kneel in shell-headed recesses separated by Ionic columns – an example of the revived Renaissance interest in the pagan culture of Ancient Greece and Rome.

The 400-year-old Mildmay tomb in Chelmsford Cathedral ▼

There is a reminder of the emptiness of worldly pomp in the tomb of Robert Cecil, Earl of Salisbury, chief minister of Elizabeth I and James I, in St Etheldreda's, Hatfield. He rests grandly in effigy on a slab of black marble supported by four kneeling female figures which represent the Virtues, but underneath lies a grisly skeleton on a humble mat of straw. An unusual 17th-century monument to Lady Margaret Hoby at Bisham does not show her at all, but only an obelisk crowned by a heart, surrounded by four marvellously carved swans, from the Hoby coat of arms. At Marlow, on the other hand, the monument of the same period to Sir Miles Hobart depicts in realistic detail the accident which killed him, when his coach overturned on Holborn Hill in London.

Perhaps the richest collection of all is in Windsor, in St George's Chapel and the Royal Mausoleum, culminating in Sir Alfred Gilbert's gigantic and overwhelmingly elaborate monument to the Duke of Clarence who died in 1892. A forgotten princeling who died young is commemorated for ever in one of the greatest artistic masterpieces in the country.

PLESHEY

MAP REF: 89TL6614

Pleshey appears to have a very long history of fortification, extending back to the Ancient Britons, who probably first laid out the 40-acre enclosure. It was improved by the Romans, but it was the Normans who created the huge motte-and-bailey castle in the 12th century. The motte is 50ft high and is approached, across a deep moat, by a 15th-century brick bridge, said to be the oldest in England. The outer bailey surrounds most of the village, creating a good impression of how many medieval villages must have appeared.

POLESDEN LACEY

MAP REF: 91TQ1452

This elegant Regency-style house with its extravagantly furnished rooms belonged, in the first half of the century, to an equally extravagant lady – the society hostess, the Hon Mrs Greville, who gave it to the National Trust in 1942. The pictures, furniture and other works of art are all a reflection of the opulence of the Edwardian era, to which Polesden Lacey is a lasting monument. There had been other houses on the site, including one owned by the playwright, Richard Brinsley Sheridan. The Duke and Duchess of York, later King George and Queen Elizabeth, spent part of their honeymoon at Polesden.

There are a number of individual gardens in what was once the walled kitchen garden, including rose, iris, rock, winter and sunken gardens. On a different scale are the lawns, with their fine beeches, cedars and limes, and the long terraced walk, where it is easy to visualise elegant men and women strolling on summer evenings. An open-air theatre was established here in 1951 and has flourished, each summer performing works from Shakespeare to Gilbert and Sullivan, not forgetting Sheridan (see page 75).

To the south is **Ranmore Common**, overlooked from the terrace and consisting of 470 acres of woodland, much of it remarkably unspoilt for commonland so close to London.

PRINCES RISBOROUGH

MAP REF: 86SP8003

This charming small town has an early 19th-century market hall but its most notable building is the elegant 17th-century redbrick

▲ Reigate Heath windmill. Its sails have been fixed and the roundhouse turned into a chapel

Manor House. Once owned by Sir Peter Lely, court painter to Charles II, the house is opened only by written appointment with the tenant. Designed in an L-shape, with a charming small courtyard, it has inside some fine panelling and a magnificent Jacobean oak staircase.

The town is overlooked by **Whiteleaf Cross**, a 30ft × 80ft cross cut in the chalk of the Chiltern downlands, its top touching the Ridgeway Path. Its origin is uncertain, but some suggest that monks from Missenden Abbey were responsible. During the 19th century the townsfolk treated the cleaning of the cross as an annual event and in 1947 it was incorporated into the arms of the county. Above it, the Whiteleaf barrow contained the body of a man when excavated in the 1930s.

REIGATE

MAP REF: 92TQ2550

The manor of Churchefelle was recorded in Domesday, and in the early 12th century Reigate Castle was built to the north of the present High Street; its earthworks are visible in the public gardens now occupying the site. Part of the castle site was destroyed in 1824, when a road tunnel was cut at the

▲ Reigate Priory, now a school, stands on the edge of Priory Park. There is a museum here

foot of Reigate Hill.

The 'new' town of Reigate grew up around the castle and although several interesting buildings survive, much of the town is modern. The 18th-century town hall is an attractively arcaded building, while Reigate Priory, originally Tudor but largely 18th-century is now a school housing the Priory Museum.

The Holmesdale Natural History

Club Museum in Croydon Road is pleasingly old-fashioned, with its local maps and other documents, photographs and a collection of stuffed birds, butterflies and insects from the area.

Nearby **Reigate Heath** is a pleasant area of heathland, copse and downland, partly owned by the National Trust. The windmill, a post mill, was built in 1765 but only worked for 15 years. The roundhouse was later converted to a chapel, but the sails and tailpole are still in position. There are seven round barrows on the heath east of the windmill, forming a Bronze Age cemetery.

RICHMOND UPON THAMES
MAP REF: 92TQ1774

There is a history of settlement in this area on the River Thames extending back to prehistoric times. Much later, royalty found Richmond congenial and so, as a result, did the rich and famous, yet Richmond remained so small and

exclusive that it did not become a borough until 1890, well after the advent of the railways had expanded its population and that of other Thames-side boroughs.

The charming oasis of Richmond Green, behind the busy shopping area, is lined with trees and surrounded by 17th- and 18th-century houses. A gateway of the original Richmond Palace faces the Green and through this is Old Palace Yard where the remains of old buildings are incorporated in more recent structures. Beyond is

▲ Richmond Park has long been famous for its red and fallow deer

Old Palace Lane, with terraced cottages running down to the river.

The views from Richmond Hill are rightly famous. At its foot is the charming village of **Petersham**, with **Ham House** by the river. Ham was built in 1610 and refurbished some 60 years later by the Duke and Duchess of Lauderdale. The outside is pleasant, but the furnishings of the rooms 'make' Ham. With very few exceptions, they are the originals, many of remarkable richness. The Lauderdales may have been singularly well matched in self-esteem, but they had taste!

Richmond Park, at 2,470 acres the largest of London's royal parks, was enclosed for hunting by Charles I in 1637 and opened to the public by William and Mary. In addition to its extensive herds of red and fallow deer, a wide range of habitats ensures that many plant and animal species thrive here. Within the park is the Isabella Plantation where displays of azaleas, rhododendrons, camellias and other flowering shrubs create colour from spring to autumn.

ROCHESTER
MAP REF: 93TQ7468

Since the road bridge carrying the M2 high over the Medway diverted traffic from Rochester, the town has tended to be ignored by many visitors to Kent. Yet this ancient settlement, inhabited since pre-Roman times, has a fine castle and cathedral, close connections with Dickens – it is featured in many of his novels – and many more attractions including its fair share of interesting shops.

Opposite the 17th-century

guildhall, where a museum is housed, is the 400-year-old Bull Hotel, which is mentioned in two of Dickens' stories. Also in the High Street is The Six Poor Travellers' House, an almshouse established here by the Richard Watts Charity, founded in 1579 to provide six bedrooms and a dining room as free accommodation for any six poor travellers, for one night only 'be they noe commen rogues or proctors' – a beneficence that continued until 1940. Predictably, Rochester has a Dickens Festival, and a Dickens Centre – an excellent museum detailing Dickens' associations with Kent.

But Rochester's most notable buildings are, undoubtedly, the castle and its neighbour, the cathedral. The Norman exterior of the cathedral has suffered from various additions and from the ravages of time, but inside, although it cannot be denied that Rochester is a mixture of styles, the quality of the work is often superb, representing the best of English cathedral architecture.

The castle's great keep is 12th-century, though an earlier fortress on the site was constructed just after the Norman Conquest. In 1215 the rebel barons lost the castle to King John, when they tried to stop him reaching London from Dover. Rochester is one of the best-preserved castles in England, and the view of the Medway from the battlements is marvellous, not least because the sense of history is almost tangible. From Hengist to Duke William, from Chaucer to Dickens, from the Pilgrims' Way to the Channel Tunnel, Kent has always been involved.

ROYAL TUNBRIDGE WELLS

MAP REF: 93TQ5839

It was Lord North who 'discovered' the waters here in 1606, but the patronage of King Charles I's wife, Henrietta Maria, established the town. After her visit to 'the Tonbridge wells' following the birth of the future Charles II, it rapidly developed as a series of settlements on the low hills. By the time Beau Nash arrived to be master of ceremonies in 1735, Tunbridge Wells had changed its name and was already a centre for 'company and diversion'. It may have lacked the grandeur of a Bath or a Buxton, but it possessed a rural charm. Architecturally, the closest Tunbridge Wells comes to Bath is on Mount Pleasant, where Decimus Burton laid out an attractive crescent and a number of villas collectively known as Calverley Estate.

The royal connection led to the building of the Church of St Charles the Martyr. Outside it is plain, apart from a charming wooden clock-turret, but inside it has the most beautiful plaster ceiling, set off by simple, dark wood galleries. The Pantiles, an elegant Regency arcade with Tuscan columns, is lined by pollarded lime trees.

The haphazard mosaic of weatherboarding, stucco, redbrick and tile-hung materials on the shop fronts, combined with classical elements, produces a lovely mixture of the sophisticated and the vernacular.

Tunbridge Wells has a fine municipal museum, marvellous parks and a cricket ground that is quintessentially English. The town is fringed by commons, encroaching almost to the centre in places. A number of rocky outcrops on the commons provide a challenge for climbers, giving visitors a further diversion.

RYE HOUSE

MAP REF: 88TL3609

A little north of Hoddesdon (see page 54) is Rye House, a small area possessing an historic 15th-century gatehouse and a small nature reserve. The gatehouse is all that remains of a moated house where a plot was hatched in 1681 by a group of Cromwellians to seize and, probably, to assassinate King Charles II as he returned from Newmarket races. The king left early, the plot was leaked and the conspirators were executed. In 1864 the gatehouse became part of a popular complex along the lines of Vauxhall Pleasure Gardens. It is now part of the Lea Valley

Regional Park and houses an exhibition.

The Royal Society for the Protection of Birds reserve at **Rye House Marsh** is only 13 acres in extent but this riverside site contains several different habitats. Intended as an educational reserve for children, it has attracted a number of relatively rare bird species, such as Cetti's warbler and bearded tit, not normally associated with urban areas. Its record and proximity to London ensures that many RSPB members visit it at weekends.

Technically, both gatehouse and reserve are in **Standstead Abbots**, a village with few claims to fame except its old Parish Church of St James. Unspoilt 15th-century, with an equally unchanged interior in the fashion of the 18th century, with whitewashed walls, high box pews, a wonderful three-decker pulpit and lots of improving texts, it is now virtually unused and in the care of the Redundant Churches Fund.

ST ALBANS

MAP REF: 87TL1407

Nowadays a flourishing commuter town, St Albans was originally Roman, but the medieval core of the present town is still reflected in its streets and alleys even if parts of the town have been modernised. The town was named after Alban, a Roman soldier

The Pantiles in Tunbridge Wells was a grassed area known as The Walks until the young Duke of Gloucester slipped and his mother complained ▼

▲ St Albans Abbey features architecture from 10 centuries

executed for sheltering a Christian priest in AD304 who was later canonised as Britain's first Christian martyr.

The abbey church was rebuilt by the first Norman abbot in the 11th century and has seen many additions – not all appropriate – over the centuries. It also suffered from neglect at various periods and in 1870 the structure was ruinous. It was saved by the future Lord Grimthorpe, a wealthy amateur architect who, at his own expense, hired Sir George Gilbert Scott to redesign the abbey church. Although this resulted in the building being saved, its Victorian west front is totally out of keeping with the rest of the structure. St Alban's became a cathedral in 1877.

Even more famous than the abbey is the archaeological site of the Roman city of Verulamium, built on Watling Street. Boudicca devastated the town 10 years or so after it had been completed, but it recovered and flourished throughout the Roman occupation of Britain. Sir Mortimer Wheeler excavated the site in the early 1930s, and much can be seen of this and subsequent excavations, on site and at the museum, including the mosaic floors which confirm how impressive the private houses must have been. The Roman theatre is not to be missed; rebuilt several times, it could probably accommodate 5–6,000 people.

Sir Francis Bacon lived near by at **Gorhambury**, in a now-ruined 16th-century manor house. Its successor, Gorhambury House, a Palladian mansion of 1784, is open to the public and contains portraits of almost all the Grimston family,

its owners for nearly 350 years.

At **Chiswell Green**, the Royal National Rose Society has its internationally famous collection of old and new roses. Over 1,000 species and some 30,000 plants are displayed daily in summer to the public.

SEVENOAKS
MAP REF: 93TQ5255

Sevenoaks, a prosperous market town by the late 12th century, has a long and remarkably tranquil history, broken only by a skirmish in which Jack Cade and his men killed 24 supporters of King Henry VI in 1405.

This mellow, charming town has a 600-year-old church where John Donne was rector for 15 years, and a public school, designed by Lord Burlington, incorporating some lovely almshouses. There are many

splendid buildings, including tile-hung cottages, and the finest of all medieval great houses, Knole (see page 58).

To the south is the 18th-century **Riverhill House**, with splendid views over the Weald from its fine, terraced garden featuring trees, azaleas and rhododendrons.

SHERE
MAP REF: 91TQ0747

In terms of visual appeal, the gem among the Tillingbourne villages is Shere, triumphing over the often disastrous tag of 'most beautiful village in Surrey'. Never lacking sightseers, Shere is best avoided in

▲ Many footpaths around Shere make exploration on foot easy

high summer, but a visit is a must. Lutyens built the lych-gate for the part-Norman church, and several other buildings in the village. Shere lies just below the Pilgrims' Way, and it is still possible to see the crosses scratched by pilgrims on the door of the church. The ages of the village houses range from the 16th-century Ash Cottage and ever-popular White Horse Inn, through a 17th-century timbered building housing the post office, to several which may not be as old as they appear, but are still picturesque and fully in keeping with the overall effect.

STANDEN
MAP REF: 92TQ3936

Standen was the last major house designed by Philip Webb, possibly the most influential of the architects who rebelled against what they saw as Victorian excesses in house building. He was a friend of William Morris, designing furniture for Morris's firm, and building his house, the Red House, at Bexleyheath.

Standen is very much as it was when built in the 1890s, carefully preserved by the two generations of the Beale family for whom it was built and who lived in it before it passed to the National Trust. Externally, the house is a rather strange mixture, with a tower, five gables, tall chimneys and some 15th-century farm buildings. It is very much in the tradition of the Arts and Crafts movement, with Webb emphasising the range of vernacular materials and styles he used – redbrick, sandstone, tile-hanging, weatherboarding, even pebble-dash. The terraced garden is not as originally planned, but it retains glorious views of the Weald.

Inside, the house is particularly light and airy, a pleasant contrast to much Victorian heaviness of the period – a contrast equally noticeable in the fittings, all designed by Webb. Standen contains many William Morris textiles and wallpapers, the majority originals, others carefully restored (see page 75).

STOKE POGES
MAP REF: 90SU9783

Stoke Poges is firmly associated with Thomas Gray, whose *Elegy in a Country Churchyard*, one of the most famous poems in the English language, is said to have been composed with the churchyard of the village Church of St Giles in mind. Naturally, there are those who make claims for other sites, but the romantic legend insists on St Giles', where Gray is buried in a simple tomb with his mother.

It was while staying with his mother that Gray composed the *Elegy* and his *Ode on a Distant Prospect of Eton College*. Mrs Gray lived with her sister in West End, now part of Stoke Court, a house built by James Wyatt. He was also responsible for Gray's Monument, erected 28 years after Gray died in Cambridge of 'severe internal gout'. This rather heavy 'classical' memorial, inscribed with words from the *Elegy*, is cared for by the National Trust.

SYON HOUSE AND PARK GARDENS
MAP REF: 92TQ1776

Syon House is a 16th-century mansion, the historic seat of the Dukes of Northumberland, standing on the banks of the River Thames between Brentford and Isleworth. The site has had a chequered history since Henry V founded a monastery here in 1415. The Duke of Somerset acquired the land after the Dissolution, building a large house before being accused of treason and executed. Lady Jane Grey was offered the Crown at Syon, reigning for just nine days. Elizabeth I granted the house to the Earls of Northumberland but the ill-fortune continued, and it was not until several generations later, when John Dudley was created Duke of Northumberland by special Act of Parliament, that Syon entered a more settled period.

▲ Beautifully furnished Syon House

Robert Adam designed the interior of the house for the Duke, and the result is a startling contrast of styles. From the outside, Syon is still a less than imposing building, its austere monastic origins apparent through 18th-century additions. Inside, the young Adam produced some of his finest and freshest work.

The Great Conservatory in Syon Park is a marvel. Over 100yds long, with acres of glass, it became the model for the Crystal Palace in the Great Exhibition of 1851. Syon boasts a six-acre rose garden, the largest garden centre in the country, an aquarium and the London butterfly house, where many rare and exotic species fly freely. In sharp contrast there is a motor museum with over 90 vehicles (see page 76).

ALONG THE ESTUARY

East of the Isle of Dogs and Greenwich, the Thames runs on towards the sea by Gravesend Reach – where the river is a mile wide between Tilbury and Gravesend – and then through the reach called the Lower Hope ('hope' in the old sense of a haven) to broaden out between Canvey Island and the Isle of Grain.

There are still extensive stretches of marshland along the banks and the falling tide reveals gleaming mudflats and sandbanks, notably the Blythe Sands along the Kentish shore east of Gravesend. This area of Kent, in the old Hundred of Hoo, is a solitary region of space and silence under huge skies. Buoys heave on the swell of the estuary and flotsam from passing ships washes up below the sea wall. The saltings are breeding grounds for multitudes of waterfowl – garganey and godwall – pochard and pintail, shelduck and shoveler. The

THORPE PARK
MAP REF: 91TQ0368

The first theme park to be established in Britain, Thorpe Park, just off the M25 near Chertsey, covers some 400 acres including extensive areas of flooded gravel pits. Transport is by train and water bus.

Over 70 attractions have been set up, including the Our Heritage section which displays life-size models depicting Vikings, Normans and other peoples who have invaded Britain. There is a street with examples of buildings from every period of British architecture and, in Model World, scale models of famous buildings such as the Eiffel Tower and the Taj Mahal. A World War I airfield, a roller-coaster, a space station and a display of sea craft add to the diversity. There are also water sports activities, including windsurfing and water-skiing.

When a period of relaxation is needed, visitors can enjoy the tranquil water garden, planted with over 50 species of trees. Alternatively, Thorpe Farm offers a craft centre where basketwork, pottery and spinning are demonstrated amid pens with farm animals. In European Square visitors can choose from a number of restaurants offering the food of various countries (see page 75).

▲ Shelduck, an estuary bird

largest heronry in Britain is at the RSPB reserve of Northward Hill.

Far down into the 19th century the villages along the Essex and Kent shores lived by fishing, using small trawlers and smacks among the mudbanks to net mackerel, sprats and whitebait. Lobster pots were set and oysters dredged up. In Victorian times Barking had a thriving trawler fleet, whose catch was brought back swiftly to port and placed on ice, obtained by flooding the marshes outside the town before the winter frosts set in.

Flat-bottomed sailing barges, called hoys, were also busy on the estuary, laden with fruit and vegetables from Essex and Kent for London. They also carried brick, timber and building stone, as well as hay and straw for London's horses, while taking back manure to spread on the fields. Until the railways came, fast sailing boats looking something like Viking longships carried passengers between Gravesend and London.

Industrialisation came to the river banks in the 19th century, following the invention of cement, which needed ready access to chalk and clay as ingredients. On the Essex side outcrops of chalk around Purfleet and Tilbury sprouted the tall chimneys of cement works. On the opposite bank the fishing village of Northfleet became the cement capital of Kent and the works there today is the biggest in Britain. Today, too, power stations and oil refineries stand like Martian invaders among the ancient marshes.

Life Museum has a collection of agricultural implements and several vernacular buildings. There is also an arboretum here with over 100 species of trees from all over the world.

The first Cistercian foundation in Britain was at Waverley Abbey, a mile north, established in 1128. It was also one of the first of the religious houses to be suppressed, in 1536. Little now remains, but excavations suggest it possessed none of the grandeur of the later, northern abbeys, like Rievaulx.

TONBRIDGE
MAP REF: 93TQ5846

Tonbridge is situated at the highest navigable point of the River Medway, and its strategic value has been recognised since the Iron Age. The Saxons built here and the Normans added an important castle. The arrival of the railways began the process of converting Tonbridge into one of the major commuter towns of the south east. It lacks the fine buildings associated with nearby Tunbridge Wells, but the ruins of the castle can still be seen, and there are several attractive houses – some incorporating stone from the castle – around the High Street.

Tonbridge Castle was begun in 1088 and substantial sections remain – the motte and bailey, lengths of curtain wall, and a magnificent round-towered gatehouse, built by Edward I. An 18th-century Gothic mansion inside the bailey now houses council offices.

Tonbridge School has produced many Kent county cricketers – the Cowdrey family were all educated here – but is a little disappointing architecturally, considering that it has been in existence since 1553.

TILBURY
MAP REF: 93TQ6476

Once a major port for ocean-going liners, the docks at Tilbury have developed as one of the most extensive container ports in Europe, bringing renewed prosperity to the town. The Thurrock Riverside Museum illustrates the way of life of local people associated with the Thames since the Bronze Age.

The late 17th-century Tilbury Fort stands on the site of an earlier fortification built by Henry VIII. Here Elizabeth I gathered her troops before the Armada, inspiring them with the speech beginning 'I know I have the body of a weak and feeble woman, but I have the heart and stomach of a king'. Charles II ordered the new fort following a raid by the Dutch up the Medway in 1667. A model of its kind, the fort had as many as 161 guns at one time, but never saw military action. It was the scene of a violent incident in 1776, when a dispute at a cricket match between Kent and Essex led to the deaths of three men, one of the Essex team and two soldiers from the fort. In World War II it served as a Home Guard base before being de-militarised in 1950.

There is a good path alongside the River Medway at Tonbridge ▶

TILFORD
MAP REF: 90SU8743

Tilford has two medieval stone bridges, one of four arches, the other with six, and two branches of the River Wey join here. The village has a large triangular green with one of Lutyens' earliest works, the Tilford Institute (1893) beside it, but the main attraction is King John's Oak, said to be 900 years old. The trunk is 26ft in diameter and the tree was described by William Cobbett as 'by far the finest tree that I ever saw in my life'.

Just outside the village, the Rural

of George II, when he was ranger here in the 1740s. The lake was fringed by follies, ruins, dams, cascades and a grotto, most of which have disappeared. The columns on the site are said to come from the Roman city of Leptis Magna in Libya.

Virginia Water has a number of gardens and collectively they form one of the great gardens of the 20th century. The **Savill Garden** was laid out in 1932. Here, rhododendrons, azaleas and lilies are much in evidence in the woodland part, but the provision of both dry and wet gardens, and an alpine meadow, allow a staggering range of plants to be featured. The **Valley Gardens**, begun after World War II, are 'natural' gardens developed in the small valleys north of Virginia Water. More rhododendrons, azaleas, flowering cherries and many species of heather are among the plants that ensure continuous colour.

TOTTERNHOE
MAP REF: 87SP9821

Totternhoe has a number of thatched and timbered buildings, including the Cross Keys Inn. There are three parts to the village, Lower End, where there was a medieval manor, Middle End, with a timber-framed house, probably 16th-century, and Church End, where the majority of the older houses are situated.

The village lies very much in the shadow of **Totternhoe Knolls**, a chalk hill topped by the mound of a Norman motte and two baileys. There are vast views from the hill which was almost certainly used as a look-out by the Saxons long before the Normans built their castle. Even earlier are the remains of fields worked by late Bronze Age and early Iron Age villagers.

The escarpment was once quarried for Totternhoe stone, long in demand for fine buildings. Windsor Castle and Westminster Abbey are early examples of its use, Ashridge one of the last. The village church, St Giles', is built of Totternhoe stone and has, scratched on its exterior walls, graffiti of medieval post mills.

TRING
MAP REF: 86SP9211

In this small market town the best houses, mostly Victorian, lie just off the High Street. Much of Tring,

▲ The Grand Union Canal near Tring is fed by the Tring reservoirs

including Tring Park, was owned by the Rothschild family from 1873 to 1938. Among their many additions is the Zoological Museum, once the private collection of the second baron and now an annexe to the Natural History Museum. Although modernised, it seems old-fashioned, perhaps due to such exhibitions as fleas clad in human clothes, part of the largest flea collection in the world!

Tring Reservoirs National Nature Reserve is about a mile north. The four reservoirs, built in the early 19th century, act as a water store for the Grand Junction Canal. The canal reaches its highest point (400ft) near by. With seven locks in the area, the passage of each boat draws some 50,000 gallons of water from the system. Large numbers of ducks overwinter on the reservoirs, with teal, wigeon, goosander and pochard joining mallard. Harriers are regular visitors as are several tern species, including black tern, in the summer. The reserve is particularly rich in marsh plants.

VIRGINIA WATER
MAP REF: 90TQ0067

This two-mile stretch of water on the edge of Windsor Great Park (see page 73) was created by William, Duke of Cumberland, son

WALTHAM ABBEY
MAP REF: 88TL3800

An example of how old and new can be mixed, Waltham Abbey has some very attractive houses, grouped around Market Square and Sun Street. Epping Forest District Museum and the library are sited in three of Sun Street's timber-framed buildings. In contrast, there is a new, pedestrianised, shopping centre and a sports centre. Recreation and relaxation is the theme of the giant **Lee Valley Regional Park**, extending north and south of the town.

The heart of Waltham is still the Abbey Church of Holy Cross, smaller now than when King Harold paid for the rebuilding of a church to house a stone crucifix

Virginia Water ▼

credited with miraculous properties. About a century later, in 1177, Henry II founded an Augustinian monastery here and pulled down the east end of Harold's church, where he was buried after the Battle of Hastings. The outline is marked out in the churchyard, with a black stone indicating Harold's burial place.

At the Dissolution, Waltham was the last of the large monasteries to surrender, but the magnificent nave survived because it belonged to the parish, not the abbey (see Dunstable, page 41). The church tower collapsed in 1552, causing extensive damage, and the church bells had to be sold to pay for repairs; over the years 13 new bells have been acquired. Much lovely stained glass in the church was lost during World War II, but Burne-Jones' good glass for the unsuitable Victorian wheel window has survived.

Of the abbey buildings, little remains but part of the 12th-century cloisters, a 14th-century gatehouse and a bridge. The town was once part of the 60,000-acre Waltham Forest, and although a great deal of the woodland of Essex *has* been lost over the centuries, this simply meant that the area came under Forest Law, and that deer were protected, not that it was a forest in the modern sense of the word (see Hatfield, page 51, and Epping, page 42).

Waltham's Abbey Church ▼

▲ The River Lea at Ware

WALTHAM CROSS
MAP REF: 88TL3600

When Edward I's Queen, Eleanor of Castile, died in Lincolnshire in 1290, her funeral cortege took 13 days to travel to Westminster Abbey, and a cross was later erected at each overnight resting place. Waltham Cross has one of only three surviving examples – the others are at Geddington and Northampton, with a replica in Charing Cross Station. Restored in 1892, Waltham's cross is now, unhappily, overshadowed by a modern shopping centre.

Waltham Cross only became a separate parish in 1855 – until then it was part of **Cheshunt**. Old Cheshunt has some pleasant buildings, including the Robert Dewhurst Free School.

Wren's Temple Bar, erected at the Fleet Street entrance to the City of London in 1672, was dismantled 200 years later and transferred to Theobalds Park, site of the great palace built by Lord Burghley in 1564 and destroyed a century later. A few tantalising fragments remain of Theobalds – so admired by James I that he exchanged it for Hatfield (see page 51). Temple Bar has been disgracefully neglected, but all attempts to return it to the City, the latest in mid-1991, have failed.

WARE
MAP REF: 88TL3514

Ermine Street crossed the River Lea at Ware, an important river port and market town from early medieval times. At Domesday Ware had two manor houses, one of which may have been Place House,

rebuilt in the 13th century – much of its great aisled hall exists today. In West Street there are the remains of a 13th-century timber-framed house. The High Street developed parallel to the River Lea and many of the 16th- and 17th-century houses have wagon entries, leading to outbuildings and the river.

Buildings like the very large Victoria Maltings are a reminder that this was a centre for the processing of barley into malt from Tudor times. The malt was shipped downstream to London breweries, while the grain marketed in Ware was sent to the mills in Stratford. On the river's edge the merchants built, in the 18th century, many attractive summerhouses or gazebos. After a period of neglect, they have been restored and are enhancing the view along the river bank.

Ware is not just an industrial centre – it has a long history. King Alfred fought a battle against the Danes at Ware in AD895 and Lady Jane Grey was proclaimed Queen here in 1533. Shakespeare mentions the Great Bed of Ware in *Twelfth Night* – after a chequered career this 11ft-square monster is now in the Victoria and Albert Museum. It spent time in several local inns, including the Saracen's Head, before being transferred to Rye House (see page 64).

In the 18th century, the Quaker poet and friend of Dr Johnson, Sir John Scott of Amwell House, Ware, devised a grotto in Scotts Road with passages lined with flints, quartz and shells. Scott's Grotto can be visited, while Amwell House is now part of Ware College.

WATFORD
MAP REF: 87TQ1196

Now the largest industrial town in Hertfordshire, the old town of Watford is not easy to locate, having been transformed last century from a one-street town to a centre for many new industries. The best of the buildings that have survived, including the 16th-century five-gabled almshouses and the early 18th-century Fuller/ Chilcott School, are to be found near the parish church. The superb museum, winner of a Museum of the Year award, is housed in a fine 18th-century house, long used by the brewers, Benskins.

Watford is well served with public parks and wooded areas, among them the three-and-a-half-acre Cheslyn Gardens combining woodland with formal planting, a rock garden and an aviary. Whippendell Woods provide 200 acres of beech, oak and hornbeam with footpaths, picnic areas and two nature trails, while Cassiobury Park once housed the seat of the Earls of Essex. Both the River Gade and the Grand Union Canal run through it.

▲ Squerryes Court at Westerham. The house was built in 1681

WESTERHAM
MAP REF: 93TQ4454

Westerham has experienced mixed fortune with transport policies in recent years. It suffered when Beeching's axe fell on the railways, but gained welcome relief when completion of the M25 eased the heavy traffic which had made its centre increasingly hazardous. Westerham has any number of pleasant vernacular houses, spreading out along the A25, but is immensely popular with tourists through its connections with General Wolfe and Winston Churchill, whose statue broods over the small, sloping green.

Wolfe, victor of the Battle of Quebec, also has a statue on the green, and was brought up in the pleasant, square, 17th-century Quebec House. It contains nothing startling, just some fine fireplaces (older than the house) and quietly appropriate furniture. The house is almost opposite the turning to Chartwell, two miles away, where Churchill lived (see page 36).

Westerham has a further treat – Squerryes Court – a William and Mary manor house, with collections of furniture, fine paintings and Wolfeiana. The Darent, once one of Kent's most charming rivers but now sadly depleted of water, rises in the lovely grounds.

A bronze statue of Churchill at Westerham. The plinth of white marble was given to the town by Marshal Tito and the people of Yugoslavia ▼

WEST MALLING
MAP REF: 93TQ6757

A market used to be held in the broad High Street of West Malling and over the centuries this large village has acquired some attractive inns and houses, including the half-timbered Priest's House, possibly 14th-century. One or two 17th-century houses and a number of good later houses, many in brick and white stucco, add to the charm. The Church of St Mary has a Norman tower and other Norman features, and some of the gravestones have grotesque carved faces. Adjoining the High Street is Manor Park Country Park, a 52-acre area with trails and a lake, near to which are the remains of an 18th-century ice house.

The impressive St Leonard's Tower, of Kentish ragstone, stands in an orchard and is believed to have been built around 1080 by Bishop Gundulf of Rochester. There is no other evidence of fortification and one theory suggests that it was intended to protect the agricultural lands of Malling Abbey, founded by the bishop at about the same time. Re-established in the 19th century by Anglican Benedictine nuns, the abbey is not accessible to the public but has the ruins of an 11th-century tower.

Beyond the nunnery is **East Malling**, where the world-famous horticultural research station occupies the old manor house in Bradbourne Park. Nearby **Offham** is of Saxon origin. It possesses an example of a medieval quintain, or tilting pole. Set on the village green, and used for practice by jousters, it provided a sporting spectacle for the villagers!

WEST WYCOMBE
MAP REF: 86SU8294

Largely owned by the National Trust, who bought it in 1929 to save it from demolition, West Wycombe village has many good 17th- and 18th-century houses and two ancient inns.

It is best known, however, for West Wycombe Park, bought by

▲ The Hell Fire Club used to meet in the golden ball on Wycombe's church

the Dashwood family towards the end of the 17th century. The first Sir Francis Dashwood built a simple brick house on the site, but the second Sir Francis rebuilt the house as it appears today. Inside, it reflects every aspect of 18th-century taste from baroque to neo-classical Roman. Paintings, sculpture and furnishings are everywhere, set in richly decorated surroundings.

The park was largely designed by Humphry Repton, with lakes, follies, temples and a cascade. The Dashwoods still live here, owning the caves and the mausoleum, next to the Church of St Lawrence. Both mausoleum and church were designed by the second Sir Francis. The mausoleum is six-sided, modelled on the Arch of

Constantine in Rome. Open to the skies, it contains monuments to family and friends. The site of the church is ancient and the present classical exterior conceals a 13th-century chancel. The silver gilt font is fascinating, a serpent curling up the stem and five doves on the bowl. The nave is huge, with 16 columns bedecked with heavy stucco leaves and flowers. The golden ball on the church tower is a notable landmark. It contains a room capable of seating eight people, and members of the Hell Fire Club (also known as the Knights of St Francis of Wycombe) are said to have dined and played cards in it (see below).

The caves contain tableaux illustrating the life and times of the second Sir Francis.

▲ Sir Francis worshipping Venus

FIRE AND BRIMSTONE

The members of Sir Francis Dashwood's so-called Hell Fire Club seem never to have used that name themselves, but it has stuck to them. A group of 24 rakes, politicians and rich men-about-town, they called themselves the Medmenham Monks or 'Franciscans', in tribute to the wild and eccentric Sir Francis, who founded the brotherhood in 1745. He took a lease on Medmenham Abbey, where the brethren gathered to dress up in monkish habits and enjoy drunken orgies with the 'nuns' they brought down from London.

Over the door of the house was inscribed a motto from Rabelais, *Fay ce que voudras* ('Do what you will'). The chapel was fitted up with pornographic pictures and there were blasphemous parodies of church services. Whether there was any serious worship of the Devil, as rumour maintained, seems extremely doubtful, but there was a famous

occasion when John Wilkes, who was briefly a member, smuggled in an ape in a long black cloak and a pair of horns. He let it loose among the cavorting 'monks' and 'nuns', and caused a panic.

Wilkes blew the whistle on the Medmenham Monks after Dashwood was appointed Chancellor of the Exchequer in 1762. Medmenham Abbey became an object of lively curiosity and Dashwood apparently transferred the orgies to the privacy of the caves at West Wycombe. He certainly spent much money equipping his stately grounds there with classical temples, rebuilding the parish church in a pagan style and accumulating a large pornographic library. He died in 1781, apparently unrepentant, at the age of 73.

WHEATHAMPSTEAD
MAP REF: 87TL1714

Between Verulamium and Baldock, where a Roman road crossed the River Lea, the attractive small town of Wheathampstead developed. The timber-framed Bull Inn sits beside a pool formed by the River Lea, and on the other side of a bridge over the river, in the High Street, is an old mill and weir.

It is likely that Julius Caesar's defeat in 54BC of the powerful Hertfordshire tribe the Catuvellauni, took place at the Devil's Dyke, on the edge of the town. Lord Brocket gave this pleasant, shaded place – thick with bluebells in spring – to the public to commemorate the coronation of King George VI and Queen Elizabeth.

On Nomansland Common a nature trail has been devised. The common is so-called because it once lay between land held by the abbeys of St Albans and Westminster.

WHIPSNADE
MAP REF: 87TL0117

The village is largely modern with comparatively few houses disposed round a huge, undulating green. Signposted from the green is the Tree Cathedral, designed in 1931 by Mr E K Blyth as a memorial to friends killed in World War I. It is laid out in a series of 'chapels', created by using some 25 species of trees.

A white lion cut in the downland turf proclaims the existence of Whipsnade Wild Animal Park, now 60 years old. The Zoological Society of London planned this zoo to take the larger mammals and some endangered species from Regent's Park. Ironically, Whipsnade is now more viable than its parent. Today, 80 per cent of the animals in the zoo have been bred here and some species have been successfully returned to the wild. Among the attractions are birds of prey and a children's zoo where young animals may be handled. Whipsnade has a very spacious feeling – it does extend over 500 acres – heightened by the views from the escarpment which are quite remarkably wide.

A short way south is the village of Studham, where the 17th-century county-wide cottage industry of straw-plaiting seems to have begun, although nearby Kensworth (see page 56) was more successful.

WHITELEY VILLAGE
MAP REF: 91TQ0962

Whiteley is the result of an original idea by William Whiteley, whose store was a feature of Bayswater for many years. He died in 1907, leaving one million pounds for the building of a retirement village.

The site chosen was on 225 acres of well-wooded land at St George's Hill, near Weybridge. In 1914 Frank Atkinson laid out the village in an octagonal shape. Other architects were then employed to produce what is, in effect, a group of almshouses. Some are single-storey, others two-storey, but all are in the same materials, redbrick and tiles, differing in design but harmonious. The site has all the amenities the villagers need – a church, chapels, post office and other shops, recreational facilities including a bar, communal rooms and a hospital.

Apart from mature trees, there are flower beds, lawns and wide avenues. Most of the houses have hanging baskets, producing a mass of colour throughout the summer. At the centre stands a statue of the founder, benignly surveying his creation.

WIMBLEDON
MAP REF: 91TQ2370

Wimbledon village, perched on its hill, is famous for lawn tennis played at the All England Club, and vies with other London villages for atmosphere and inhabitants – many well-known in artistic, literary or theatrical circles. It has pretty byways with charming artisan cottages, and grander Georgian and Victorian villas. Naturally it also has antique shops, boutiques, bistros and restaurants.

All this is a far cry from the more prosaic suburb of Wimbledon down the hill and, as with many rural villages, the gulf between the two is considerable. On the morning of the Cup Final which Wimbledon won, a radio poll revealed that the majority of people 'up the hill' were not aware 'their' team was even playing!

But Wimbledon has much more than sport to offer. Its large and historic common, only taken into public control in 1871, has a windmill and an Iron Age fort. Tracts of open heathland are home to skylark and yellowhammer, while in summer the scrub areas shelter whitethroat and willow warbler. Oak and birch woodland and boggy pools add to the habitats and to the opportunity to study many different species of plants and mammals. Cannizaro House on the edge of the common is now an hotel, but its park is open to the public and has flower gardens and many beautiful trees.

The Lawn Tennis Museum in

◄ Wimbledon fortnight at the end of June is a national event followed by millions. The statue below is of Fred Perry, three times champion ▼

▲ Windsor Castle has been one of the principal residences of the kings and queens of England since the reign of William the Conqueror

Church Road describes the history of tennis and displays trophies and films of famous matches.

WINDSOR

MAP REF: 90SU9576

Windsor Castle began when William the Conqueror decided that the western approach to London needed protection. The chosen site was superb, a steep chalk cliff overlooking the Thames. The first building was probably a wooden stronghold, replaced by stone in the 12th century. Added to and strengthened by successive monarchs, it is the largest castle in Europe, covering 13 acres. George IV spent a million pounds on the State Apartments alone. These fascinating rooms contain a potted history of interior decoration from the 17th to the 19th century.

Ten kings and queens are buried in St George's Chapel, where the Knights of the Most Noble Order of the Garter, Britain's premier order of knighthood, worship each June with their sovereign; their banners hang above the choir stalls. In Queen Mary's Doll's House, the work of Lutyens, the electricity and plumbing work and the books are by contemporary authors.

The exhibition of drawings, changed periodically, gives a glimpse into the richness of the Queen's private collection.

The town grew up around the castle walls, nestling into their curves for security. Today it has a full complement of antique shops, boutiques, museums and exhibitions, including the Royal Mews Exhibition, with its collection of royal carriages and coaches – some of which carry the royal party to Ascot each June (see page 52). Worth seeking out in the town are the town hall, the Market Cross House and the Shambles. Eton (see page 43) is just across the river.

Windsor Great Park is a vestige of the royal hunting forest that occupied most of medieval southern Berkshire (see also Virginia Water, page 68). The Long Walk was planted by Charles II and renewed in 1945. It stretches for three miles from the castle to a statue of George III on horseback – very appropriately, as the park is now used for many events with an equestrian flavour.

Windsor Safari Park is home to some of the world's largest mammals. Visitors drive for a mile through attractive reserves containing lions, tigers, elephants, bears and the ever-inquisitive baboons. There are many other amusements and displays to interest all ages.

WISLEY

MAP REF: 91TQ0659

Wisley is a good example for those who garden with less than perfect soil or weather conditions. It has a frost pocket and is built on sandy soil, fast draining, with a yearly rainfall which is not excessive. Yet despite all these drawbacks, a vast variety of plants has been successfully grown here for nearly 90 years. The gardens are owned by the Royal Horticultural Society and consist of about 250 acres of tree, shrub and flower garden, with vegetable gardens, farm and woodland.

The fascination of Wisley lies in its sheer range. There are trial areas, gardens for small houses, rockeries, a landscaped lake, pinetum, heather and peat gardens and several glasshouses where exotic plants from many countries are grown. The large garden centre has a fine selection of books covering every aspect of natural history and there is a gift shop, restaurant and cafeteria.

Wisley, home of the Royal Horticultural Society's experimental gardens ▼

◄ Mill End, Hambledon

The following list is just a selection of the numerous places of interest in the area around London.

The details given are intended to provide a rough guide only to opening times. Very often a place may only open for part of a day or close for lunch. Also, although stated as open all year, many places close over Christmas and New Year and some bank holidays. Full information should be obtained in advance of a visit, from the nearest tourist information centre (see page 79).

Many places are owned by either the National Trust or are in the care of English Heritage, and if this is the case the entry is accompanied by the abbreviation NT or EH.

Telephone numbers are given in brackets.

BH = bank holiday
Etr = Easter

FACT FILE

CONTENTS

Places to Visit
Stately homes, castles, gardens, theme parks, museums and other attractions

Sports and Activities
Angling, boating and river trips, cycling, golf, horse racing, motor racing, walking and the countryside, watersports

Useful Information
Addresses, tourist information centres

Customs and Events
A calendar of festivals

ASH VALE
RAMC Historical Museum, Keogh Barracks. *Exhibition of history of Royal Army Medical Corp.* Open all year, Mon to Fri, except BH.

AYLESBURY
Buckinghamshire County Museum, St Mary's Square, Church St. *Old parish rooms house local history and temporary exhibitions.* Open all year, Mon to Sat.

AYOT ST LAWRENCE
Shaw's Corner (NT). *George Bernard Shaw's house.* Open Apr to Oct, Wed to Sun and BH.

BEACONSFIELD
Bekonscot Model Village, Warwick Rd, New Town. *The world's oldest model village.* Open Mar to early Nov, daily.

BELTRING
Whitbread Hop Farm. *Restored oast-houses, museum of rural crafts and shire horses.* Open early Mar to late Nov, daily.

BERKHAMSTED
Berkhamsted Castle (EH). *Impressive castle remains.* Open all year, daily.

BEXLEY
Hall Place, Bourne Rd. *House and topiary garden.* Open all year, daily.

BOOKHAM, GREAT

Polesden Lacey (NT). *Regency house containing Greville collection.* Open Mar to Nov, Wed to Sun. Grounds open all year, daily.

BOROUGH GREEN

Great Comp Garden. *The garden has been created over the last 34 years.* Open Apr to Oct, daily.

BRASTED

Emmetts Garden, Ide Hill. *Hillside shrub garden.* Open late Mar to Oct, Wed to Sun and BH.

BRENTFORD

Kew Bridge Steam Museum, The Pumping Station, Green Dragon La. *Working steam engines.* Open all year, daily.

Musical Museum, 368 High St. *Musical machines.* Open Apr to Oct, Sat and Sun.

CHALFONT ST GILES

Chiltern Open Air Museum, Newlands Park, Gorelands La. *Traditional Chiltern buildings rebuilt.* Open early Mar to late Oct, Wed to Sun and BH.

Milton's Cottage, Dean Way. *Sixteenth-century cottage where Milton lived and worked.* Open Mar to Oct, Tue to Sun and BH.

CHARLWOOD

Gatwick Zoo & Aviaries, Russ Hill. *Mammals and birds in natural settings.* Open Mar to Oct, daily; Nov to Mar, weekends and school hols.

CHARTWELL

Chartwell. *The former home of Sir Winston Churchill.* House open Mar to Nov; gardens Apr to Oct, Tue to Thu, Sat, Sun and BH.

CHENIES

Chenies Manor. *Elizabethan manor house.* Open Apr to Oct, Mon, Wed and Thu.

CHERTSEY

Chertsey Museum, The Cedars, 33 Windsor St. *Georgian house containing costume exhibition.* Open all year, Tue to Sat.

Thorpe Park, Staines Rd. *Over 70 attractions in 500 acres.* Open late Mar to late Oct.

CHESSINGTON

Chessington World of Adventures. *Rides and attractions.* Open early Mar to Oct, daily. Zoological garden open all year, daily.

CHIDDINGSTONE

Chiddingstone Castle. *Seventeenth-century house rebuilt as a castle.* Open Apr to Oct, Sat and Sun; May to Sep, Wed to Sun and BH.

CHISLEHURST

Chislehurst Caves. Old Hill. *Labyrinth of caves.* Open Etr to Sep, daily; Sep to Etr, Sat and Sun only.

CHISWICK

Chiswick House. Burlington La. *Fine Palladian mansion.* Open all year, daily.

Hogarth House, Chiswick Flyover. *William Hogarth's former house.* Open Apr to Sep, daily.

COBHAM (KENT)

Cobham Hall. *Beautiful house set in 150 acres.* Open Mar, Apr, Jul and Aug, various days.

Owletts (NT). Charles II house. *Open Apr to Sep, Wed and Thu.*

COLINDALE (HENDON)

Royal Air Force Museum, Grahame Park Way, Hendon. *Over 60 historic aircraft.* Open all year, daily.

COMPTON

Watts Picture Gallery and Chapel, Down La. *Dedicated to the work of Victorian artist G F Watts.* Open all year, Fri to Wed.

CRAYFORD

Craft Centre of Silk, Bourne Rd. *Silk mill and museum of silk.* Open all year, daily, except BH.

DARTFORD

Dartford Museum, Market St. *Changing exhibitions of local interest.* Open all year, Mon, Tue and Thu to Sat.

Stone Lodge Farm Park, London Rd, Stone. *Working farm with heavy horses and rare breeds.* Open early Mar to late Oct, daily.

DORKING

Dorking and District Museum, The Old Foundry, West St. *Local history.* Open all year, Wed, Thu and Sat.

DORNEY

Dorney Court. *Fine Tudor manor house.* Open Etr to May, Sun and BH; Jun to Sep, Sun to Tue.

DOWNE

Darwin Museum, Down House, Luxted Rd. *Darwin collection in his former home.* Open Mar to Jan, Wed to Sun and BH Mon.

EAST CLANDON

Hatchlands (NT). *Adam decorated, 18th-century house; collection of keyboard instruments.* Open Apr to late Oct, Tue to Thu and Sun; also BH and Sat in Aug.

EAST GRINSTEAD

Standen (NT). *Philip Webb house with Morris furnishings.* Open Apr to Oct, Wed to Sun and BH.

ENFIELD

Forty Hall Museum, Forty Hill. *Seventeenth-century mansion.* Open all year, Tue to Sun.

ESHER

Claremont Landscape Garden (NT). *Earliest English landscape garden.* Open all year, daily.

EYNSFORD

Eynsford Castle (EH). *Remains of 11th-century castle.* Open Etr to Sep, daily; Sep to Etr, Tue to Sun.

Lullingstone Castle. *House altered in Queen Anne's time; beautiful grounds.* Open Apr to Oct, Sat, Sun and BH.

Lullingstone Roman Villa (EH). *Villa dating from first century; fine mosaics.* Open Etr to Sep, daily; Sep to Etr, Tue to Sun.

FARNHAM

Birdworld & Underwater World, Holt Pound. *Eighteen acres of garden with aviaries and aquarium.* Open all year, daily.

Farnham Castle Keep (EH). *Castle remains dating from 11th century.* Open Etr to Sep, daily.

Farnham Museum, 38 West St. *Georgian house containing the story of Farnham.* Open all year, Tue to Sat.

GODALMING

Godalming Museum. 109A High St. *Local history and garden.* Open all year, Tue to Sat.

Winkworth Arboretum (NT). *Hillside woodland.* Open all year, daily.

GOUDHURST

Bedgebury National Pinetum. *Conifers laid out in 160 acres.* Open all year, daily.

Finchcocks. *Keyboard instruments in Georgian house.* Open Etr to Jul and Sep, Sun; Aug, Wed to Sun. Also BH. Apr to Oct open by appointment.

GRAVESEND

Gravesham Museum, High St. *Local history.* Open all year, Mon, Tue and Thu to Sat.

GRAYS

Thurrock Museum, Orsett Rd. *Local history, agriculture and archaeology.* Open all year, Mon to Sat, except BHs.

GREENWICH

Cutty Sark Clipper Ship, Greenwich Pier. *The fastest clipper ship.* Open all year, daily.

Gipsy Moth IV, Greenwich Pier. *Yacht sailed single-handed round the world.* Open Apr to Oct, daily.

Greenwich Park. *Formal gardens, deer park and children's playground.* Open all year, daily.

National Maritime Museum, Romney Rd. *The story of Britain and the sea.* Open all year, daily.

Old Royal Observatory, Greenwich Park. *Collection of historic time-keeping, and navigational instruments.* Open all year, daily.

The Queen's House, Romney Rd. *England's first Palladian-style villa designed by Inigo Jones.* Open all year, daily. Closed some BHs.

Royal Naval College. *Painted Hall and Chapel.* Open all year, Fri to Wed.

GUILDFORD

Guildford Castle. *Three-storey, 12th-century castle keep with gardens.* Grounds open all year. Keep May to Sep, daily.

Guildford Museum, Castle Arch. *Local history.* Open all year, Mon to Sat.

Loseley House. *Elizabethan house with farm.* Open May to Oct, Wed to Sat, also BH.

HAMPSTEAD

Fenton House (NT), Windmill Hill. *Seventeenth-century mansion with collection of early keyboard instruments.* Open Apr to Oct, Sat to Wed and weekends in Mar.

Freud Museum, 20 Maresfield Gds. *Freud's home with artefacts, his work and collections.* Open all year, Wed to Sun.

Keats House, Keats Grove. *Former home of the poet, now a museum.* Open all year, daily.

Kenwood, Hampstead La. *Mansion on Hampstead Heath. Summer concerts held here.* Open all year, daily.

HAMPTON COURT

Hampton Court Palace. *Sixteenth-century palace and gardens.* Open all year, daily.

HARLOW

Harlow Museum, Passmores House, Third Av. *Georgian house set in gardens; local history exhibition.* Open all year, Mon to Fri.

Mark Hall Cycle Museum and Gardens, Muskham Rd. *The history of the bicycle, and walled gardens.* Open all year, daily.

HATFIELD

Hatfield House. *Jacobean mansion with great park, also collections of vintage cars and model soldiers.* Open late Mar to early Oct. House Tue to Sun and BH. Gardens daily.

Mill House Museum and Mill. *Mill Green.* Open all year, Tue to Sat.

HAXTED

Haxted Watermill & Museum. *Sixteenth-century mill with working wheels.* Open Apr to Sep, Wed, Sat, Sun and BH.

HENDON

Church Farm House Museum, Greyhound Hill. *Seventeenth-century house with exhibits of local interest.* Open all year, daily.

HENLEY

Fawley Court. Open Mar to Nov, Wed, Thu and Sun.

Greys Court. Open Apr to Sep, Mon, Wed and Fri. Gardens open Sat also.

HEVER

Hever Castle and Gardens, nr Edenbridge. *Romantic childhood home of Anne Boleyn.* Open mid-Mar to early Nov, daily.

HIGH WYCOMBE

Wycombe Local History and Chair Museum, Castle Hill House, Priory Ave. *Exhibition of the history, crafts and industry of the area.* Open all year, Mon to Sat.

HODDESDON

Lowewood House. High St. *Museum.* Open all year, Tue to Sat.

HUGHENDEN

Hughenden Manor (NT). *Benjamin Disraeli's house and garden.* Open Mar, Sat to Sun; Apr to Oct, Wed to Sun.

IGHTHAM

Ightham Mote (NT). *Medieval manor house with moat and garden.* Open late Mar to Oct, Sun, Mon and Wed to Fri, and BH.

ISLEWORTH

Heritage Motor Museum, Syon Park. *Over 100 vehicles telling the story of the British motor industry.* Open all year, daily.

Syon House. *Mansion with interior by Robert Adam.* Open Apr to Sep, Sun to Thu; Oct, Sun only.

Syon Park. *Landscape garden of 55 acres by Capability Brown.* Open all year, daily.

KEW

Kew Gardens (Royal Botanic Gardens). *World-famous gardens and botanical collection.* Open all year, daily.

Kew Palace, Royal Botanic Gardens. *Former country residence of Hanoverian kings.* Open Apr to Sep, daily.

Queen Charlotte's Cottage, Royal Botanic Gardens. *Eighteenth-century rustic cottage used as summerhouse.* Open Apr to Sep, Sat, Sun and BH.

KNEBWORTH

Knebworth House, Gardens & Country Park. *Stately home, fine park and gardens.* Open mid-Mar to mid-May, Sat, Sun and BH; mid-May to early Sep, Tue to Sun and BH.

LAMBERHURST

Bayham Abbey (EH), 2m W. *Ruins in wooded valley.* Open Etr to Sep, daily.

Owl House, 1m NE. *Small, timber-framed house with lovely 13-acre garden.* Open all year, daily.

Scotney Castle Garden (NT), 1m SE. *Beautiful, magical gardens around an old moated castle.* Open Apr to early Nov, Wed to Sun.

LEATHERHEAD

Leatherhead Museum of Local History, Hampton Cottage, 64 Church St. *Seventeenth-century cottage and garden with local history.* Open Apr to Dec, Fri and Sat.

LUTON

Luton Hoo (The Wernher Collection). *Art treasures collection in Adam house surrounded by 1,500* *acres.* Open late Mar to mid-Oct, Tue to Sat and BH.

Luton Museum and Art Gallery, Wardown Park. *Local and natural history.* Open all year, daily.

MAIDENHEAD

Courage Shire Horse Centre, Cherry Garden La. *Up to 12 shire horses in beautiful location.* Open Mar to Oct, daily.

MIDDLE CLAYDON

Claydon House (NT). *Eighteenth-century house with rococo state rooms.* Open Apr to Oct, Sat to Wed and BH.

OSTERLEY

Osterley Park House (NT). *Eighteenth-century villa, interior by Adam.* Park open all year, daily. House open Mar to Oct, Wed to Sun and BH; Nov to Dec, Sat and Sun.

PAINSHILL PARK

Painshill Park. *Eighteenth-century landscaped garden by Charles Hamilton.* Open mid-Apr to mid-Oct, Sun.

PENSHURST

Penshurst Place. *Grand house, park and gardens; also toy museum and adventure playground.* Open late Mar to late Sep, Tue to Sun and BH.

PLAXTOL

Old Soar Manor (EH & NT). *Built by the Culpepper family in 1290.* Open Etr to Sep, daily.

REIGATE

Priory Museum, Reigate Priory School, Bell St. *Small museum with changing exhibitions.* Open term time, Wed and first Sat in month.

RICHMOND

Ham House. *Seventeenth-century house and garden; annex of V & A.* Gardens open all year, Tue to Sun. House open Apr to Sep, Tue to Sun.

ROCHESTER

Charles Dickens Centre, Eastgate House, High St. *Fine Tudor building with the life, times and characters of Dickens.* Open all year, daily.

Guildhall Museum, High St. *Exhibits of local history etc.* Open all year, daily.

Rochester Castle (EH). *Norman castle with remarkable keep.* Open Etr to Oct, daily; Oct to Etr, closed Mon.

The Six Poor Traveller's House, High St. *Old almshouse.* Open Mar to Oct, Tue to Sat.

ROYAL TUNBRIDGE WELLS

A Day at the Wells, Corn Exchange, The Pantiles. *Reconstruction of 18th-century Tunbridge Wells.* Open all year, daily.

Tunbridge Wells Museum & Art Gallery, Civic Centre. *Local history, Tunbridge ware and temporary art exhibitions.* Open all year, Mon to Sat, except BH.

ST ALBANS

Clock Tower, Market Pl. *Fifteenth-century curfew tower.* Open Etr to mid-Sep, Sat, Sun and BH.

The Gardens of the Rose (Royal National Rose Society), Chiswell Green. *Over 1,650 varieties of rose.* Open mid-Jun to mid-Oct, daily.

Gorhambury House. *Eighteenth-century house with portrait collection.* Open May to Sep, Thu.

Kingsbury Watermill Museum, Saint Michael's St. *Sixteenth-century mill with working waterwheel.* Open all year, Wed to Sun.

Museum of St Albans, Hatfield Rd. *Local history, craft tools and workshops.* Open all year, daily.

Roman Theatre of Verulamium, St Michaels. *Roman theatre excavated and restored.* Open all year, daily.

St Albans Organ Museum, 320 Camp Rd. *Collection of automatically controlled organs.* Open all year, daily.

Verulamium Museum, St Michaels. *Remains and exhibits in 100-acre park.* Open Apr to Feb, daily.

SEVENOAKS

Knole (NT). *One of the largest houses in England.* Open late Mar to Oct, Wed to Sun and BH.

Riverhill House. Open Apr to Jun, Sun; also BH weekends.

Sevenoaks Museum, The Library, Buckhurst La. *Local history.* Open all year, Mon to Sat.

SHERE

The Shere Museum, The Malt House. *Victorian bygones.* Open all year, Mon, Tue, Thu and Fri; Etr to Sep, Sun and BH also.

STONOR

Stonor House, Stonor Park, nr Henley. *House in wooded deer park.* Open Apr to Sep on varying days.

STRATFORD

Passmore Edwards Museum, Romford Rd. *Victorian house with museum of Essex and Greater London.* Open all year, Wed to Sun and BH.

STROOD

Temple Manor (EH), Knight Rd. *Built by the Knights Templar in 1240.* Open Etr to Sep, daily.

TAPLOW

Cliveden (NT). *375 acres of garden and parkland.* Open Mar to Dec, daily. The house, now a hotel, open late Apr to Oct, Thu and Sun.

TILBURY

Thurrock Riverside Museum, Tilbury Leisure Centre, Civic Sq. *History of the River Thames.* Open all year, daily.

Tilbury Fort (EH). *Fort built by Henry VIII.* Open Etr to Sep, daily; Oct to Etr, Tue to Sun.

TILFORD

Rural Life Museum, Reeds Rd. *Farm implements displayed in old farm buildings and 10 acres of grounds.* Open Apr to Sep, Wed to Sun and BH.

TONBRIDGE

Tonbridge Castle Grounds. *Thirteenth-century gatehouse and remains.* Open all year, daily.

TOTTENHAM

Bruce Castle Museum, Lordship La. *Elizabethan house with later additions in small park.* Open all year, daily.

TRING

Zoological Museum, Akeman St. *Large collection of rare specimens.* Open all year, daily.

TWICKENHAM

Marble Hill House, Richmond Rd. *Palladian house with Georgian interior.* Open all year, daily.

Orleans House Gallery, Riverside. *Temporary exhibitions throughout the year.* Open all year, Tue to Sun and BH.

Rugby Football Union, Rugby Rd. *Tours of ground and museum.* Tours all year, Mon to Fri.

▲ Indian elephants at Whipsnade Wild Animal Park in Bedfordshire

WALTHAM ABBEY

Epping Forest District Museum, Sun St. Open all year, Fri to Tue.

Hayes Hill Farm, Stubbins Hill La. *Traditional-style farmyard and barn.* Open all year, daily.

Waltham Abbey Gatehouse, Bridge & Entrance to Cloisters. *Ruins of abbey buildings.* Open all year, daily.

WALTHAMSTOW

Vestry House Museum, Vestry Rd. *Former workhouse exhibiting items of local interest.* Open all year, Mon to Sat, except BH.

William Morris Gallery, Forest Rd. *Exhibition of work by Morris and followers in his former house.* Open all year, Tue to Sat and first Sun in month.

WARE

Scott's Grotto, Scott's Rd. Open Apr to Sep, Sat and BH.

WATFORD

Watford Museum, 194 High St. *Art gallery and museum with special wartime section.* Open all year, Mon to Sat.

WEST CLANDON

Clandon Park (NT). *Eighteenth-century house with Regimental museum.* Open Apr to Oct, Sat to Wed and BH.

WESTERHAM

Quebec House (NT). *Wolfe museum in his birthplace.* Open late Mar to Oct, Sun to Wed and Fri.

Squerryes Court. *Fine 17th-century manor house.* Open Apr to Sep, Wed, Sat and Sun.

WEST MALLING

St Leonard's Tower. *Fine early Norman tower.* Open all year, daily.

WEST WYCOMBE

West Wycombe Caves. *Caves dug by Sir Francis Dashwood and reputedly used by the Hell Fire Club.* Open Mar to Oct, daily.

West Wycombe Park (NT). *Palladian house and park built for Sir Francis Dashwood.* House and grounds open Jul to Aug, Sun to Thu. Grounds only, Apr to May, Sun and Wed, also Etr and BH.

WEYBRIDGE

Brooklands Museum, Brooklands Rd. *Motor racing and aviation exhibition.* Open all year, Sat and Sun.

WHIPSNADE

Whipsnade Wild Animal Park. *Over 2,500 animals in 600-acre park.* Open all year, daily.

WIMBLEDON

The Wimbledon Lawn Tennis Museum, Church Rd. *The story of tennis.* Open all year, Tue to Sun.

WINDSOR

Exhibition of The Queen's Presents and Royal Carriages, Windsor Castle. Open all year, daily.

Frogmore House, Home Park. *Seventeenth-century house built by Charles II's architect.* Open early Aug to Sep, Wed to Sun.

Household Cavalry Museum, St Leonards Rd. *Military collection from 1600 to present.* Open all year, Mon to Fri, except BH.

Queen Mary's Dolls' House, Windsor Castle. *Dolls' house with contents and Old Master drawings.* Open all year, daily.

Royalty and Empire Exhibition, Windsor and Eton Central Station. *Waxworks recreate Queen Victoria's Diamond Jubilee in 1897.* Open all year, daily, except part Jan.

St George's Chapel. *Fine example of Perpendicular architecture.* Open all year, daily, with exceptions.

Savill Garden, Windsor Great Park. *Twenty acres of woodland garden.* Open all year, daily.

State Apartments, Windsor Castle. *Sixteen State Rooms full of art treasures.* Open all year, daily, except when H M The Queen in residence.

Valley Gardens, Windsor Great Park. *300 acres of woodland near Virginia Water.* Open all year, daily.

Windsor Castle. *The official residence of H M The Queen; covers 13 acres.* Castle precincts open all year, daily.

Windsor Safari Park, Winkfield Rd. *African Adventure and other attractions.* Open all year, daily.

WING

Ascott House (NT). *Outstanding contents and 12-acre garden.* Open Apr to Sep at varying times.

WISLEY

Wisley Gardens. *RHS experimental gardens covering 300 acres.* Open all year, Mon to Sat; members Sun.

SPORTS AND ACTIVITIES

The following information is by no means comprehensive and further details can be obtained from the authorities and contacts given.

ANGLING

There are a number of good sites offering coarse and game fishing around London, and three water authorities concern the would-be fisherman.

Anglian Water Plc (Essex, Beds and part of Bucks), Anglian House, Ambury Road, Huntingdon, Cambs PE18 6NZ (0480 433433), Southern Water Plc (Sussex and Kent), Southern House, Worthing, West Sussex BN13 3NX (0903 64444), and Thames Water Utilities Ltd (the Thames and its tributaries), Nugent House, Vastern Road, Reading, Berks RG1 8DB (0734 593333).

The relevant authority must be approached for a rod licence before fishing in freshwater. Full details of where to fish can be obtained from these authorities. Day permits are available at several of the large reservoirs in the area.

BOATING AND RIVER TRIPS

This is a selection of the numerous places offering river trips or boats for hire around London.

Berkhamsted, *Bridgewater Boats,* Castle Wharf (0442 863615). Boats for hire on the Grand Union.

Bray, *Showboat,* Weir Bank (0628 770011). Cruises on a paddle steamer.

Chatham, *Invicta Line Cruises,* Strood Pier and Sun Pier (0634 723619). A cruise ship running across to Southend.

Kingswear Castle Paddle Steamer Trips, The Historic Dockyard (0634 827648). Trips on a vintage river paddle steamer.

Cookham, *Classic Cruisers,* Whytegates House, Berries Rd (06285 21189). Restored Edwardian launch for private hire.

Datchet, *Kris Cruisers,* The Waterfront, Southlea Rd (0753 584866). Rowing boats, hire cruisers and electric Edwardian lady craft.

Gravesend, *Lower Thames and Medway Passenger Boat Co* (0474 568038). Trips up to sights in central London.

Guildford, *Guildford Boat House,* Millbrook (0483 504494). Rowing boats, river trips, narrowboat holidays.

Henley, *Hobbs & Sons Ltd,* Station Rd (0491 572035). Cruisers for hire and trips on Thames.

Kingston-upon-Thames, *Turks Launches,* Thames Side (081 546 2434). Trips to Hampton Court and Richmond.

Marlow, *River Days,* Bridge Close, Riverside (06284 72805). Luxury day cruises on vintage Edwardian launch.

Old Windsor, *French Bros & Windsor Boats,* The Runnymead Boat House, Windsor Rd (0753 851900). Public trips and charter.

Sawbridge, *Adventuress Cruises,* Unit X, The Maltings, Station Rd (0279 600848). Trips in fully enclosed boat on Lee & Stort.

Watford, *Arcturus,* Cassio Wharf (043871 4528). Narrowboat trips on Grand Union Canal.

CYCLING

There are a number of places throughout the area where bicycles can be hired, and the Cyclists' Touring Club can provide a comprehensive list of these for the whole of Britain. Their address is Cotterell House, 69 Meadrow, Godalming, Surrey GU7 3HS (0483 417217).

GOLF

There are too many golf courses and clubs in the area covered by this book to list here, but the AA's *Guide to Golf Courses in Britain* (updated annually) gives full details of courses and their facilities.

HORSE RACING

There is racing at Ascot, Epsom, Kempton Park, Sandown and Windsor.

The International Racing Bureau, Alton House, 117 High Street, Newmarket, Suffolk CB8 9AG (0638 668881), will supply information on all aspects of racing.

MOTOR RACING

Brands Hatch, on the A20 between Swanley and Wrotham, is Britain's most well-known circuit and offers a programme of events to suit every taste in motor sport. Information can be obtained on (0474 872331).

WALKING AND THE COUNTRYSIDE

The counties around London are well served with footpaths, commons, heathland and country parks, most of which are suitable for activities such as walking, riding and bird-watching. Many of the country parks have nature trails and interpretative centres, and full details of these can be obtained from the nearest tourist board or information centre. Often County Councils run guided walks and organise a programme of countryside events.

For information about local footpaths and group outings, contact The Ramblers' Association, 1/5 Wandsworth Road, London SW8 2XX (071 582 6878).

WATERSPORTS

To obtain information about the numerous opportunities for water recreation in the area, ranging from sailing to waterskiing, contact The Water Services Association, 1 Queen Anne's Gate, London SW1H 9BT (071 222 8111).

USEFUL INFORMATION

ADDRESSES

English Heritage (EH)
Essex & Hertfordshire, 24 Brooklands Avenue, Cambridge CB2 2BU (0223 455532).

London, Hampshire, Kent, Surrey and Sussex, Spur 17, Government Buildings, Hawkenbury, Tunbridge Wells, Kent TN2 5AQ (0892 548166)

London Historic Houses, The Iveagh Bequest, Kenwood, Hampstead Lane, London NW3 7JR (081 348 1286).

Berkshire, Bridge House, Clifton, Bristol BS8 4XA (0272 734472)

The National Trust (NT)
London Office, 36 Queen Anne's Gate, London SW1H 9AS (071 222 9251).

Southern, Polesden Lacey, Dorking, Surrey RH5 6BD (0372 453401).

Kent & East Sussex, The Estate Office, Scotney Castle, Lamberhurst, Tunbridge Wells, Kent TN3 8JN (0892 890651).

Thames & Chilterns, Hughenden Manor, High Wycombe, Bucks HP14 4LA (0494 528051).

TOURIST INFORMATION

British Tourist Authority
Thames Tower, Black's Road, Hammersmith, London W6 9EL (071 730 3488).

Regional Tourist Boards
London Tourist Board, 26 Grosvenor Gardens, London SW1W 0DU (071 730 3450).

South East England Tourist Board, The Old Brew House, Warwick Park, Tunbridge Wells, Kent TN2 5TA (0892 540766).

Thames and Chilterns Tourist Board, The Mount House, Church Green, Witney, Oxon OX8 6DZ (0993 778800).

Local Tourist Information Centres
The Centres marked with an asterisk are not open all the year round.

Aldershot, Military Museum, Queens Av (0252 20968).

Aylesbury, County Hall, Walton St (0296 382308).

Bishop's Stortford, The Council Offices, 2 The Causeway (0279 655261).

Borehamwood, Civic Offices, Elstree Way (081 207 2277).

Bracknell, Central Library, Town Sq (0344 423149).

Chelmsford, County Hall, Market Rd (0245 283400).

Cranbrook*, Vestry Hall, Stone St (0580 712538).

Croydon, Katherine St (081 760 5630).

Dartford, Home Gardens (0322 343243).

Dunstable, The Library, Vernon Pl (0582 471012).

Farnham, Vernon House, 28 West St (0252 715109).

Fleet, Gurkha Sq, Fleet Rd (0252 811151).

Greenwich, 46 Greenwich Church St (081 858 6376).

Guildford, The Undercroft, 72 High St (0483 444007).

Harrow, Civic Centre, Station Rd (081 424 11032).

Heathrow Airport, Underground Station Concourse (071 730 3488).

Hemel Hempstead, Pavilion Box Office, Marlowes (0442 64451).

Henley-on-Thames*, Town Hall, Market Pl (0491 578034).

High Wycombe, 6 Cornmarket (0494 421892).

Kingston-upon-Thames, Museum & Heritage Centre, Wheatfield Way (081 546 5386).

Lewisham, Lewisham Library, 366 Lewisham High St (081 690 8325).

Luton, Grosvenor House, 45–47a Alma St (0582 401579).

Luton Airport, Main Terminal (0582 405100).

Maidenhead, The Library, St Ives Rd (0628 781110).

Redbridge, Town Hall, High Rd (081 478 3020).

Richmond, Old Town Hall, Whittaker Ave (081 940 9125).

Rickmansworth, 46 High St (0923 776611).

Rochester, Eastgate Cottage, High St (0634 843666).

St Albans, Town Hall, Market Pl (0727 864511).

Sevenoaks, Buckhurst La (0732 450305).

Tonbridge, Tonbridge Castle, Castle St (0732 770929).

Tower Hamlets, Mayfield House, Cambridge Heath Rd (081 980 4831).

Tunbridge Wells, Monson House, Monson Way (0892 515675).

Twickenham, Civic Centre, 44 York St (081 891 7272).

Windsor, Central Station, Thames St (0753 852010).

CUSTOMS AND EVENTS

Although the events shown in this section usually take place in the months under which they appear, the actual dates of many vary from year to year. Numerous other local events crop up regularly and full details of these can be obtained from tourist information centres or local newspapers.

JANUARY

Dicing for the Maid's Money
Guildford (Last Thu)
Two maids cast lots for a pension.

Wassailing
Guildford (6th). *Morris Men tour the pubs performing a mummers' play.*

MAY

May Celebrations
St Martha's Hill, nr Guildford (1st). *Morris dancing.*

May Celebrations
Guildford town centre (Sat nearest the 1st). *Dancing round the Summer Pole.*

Swearing on the Horns
Ye Old Wrestlers Tavern, Highgate (Wed preceding BH and in Sep). *Kissing and swearing on horns.*

Weighing of the Mayor
High Wycombe (end of the month). *Colourful ceremony during which the mayor is weighed.*

JUNE

Dunmow Flitch Trials
Great Dunmow (held every leap year). *A flitch of bacon is given to the couple who can prove they do not repent of their marriage after a year and a day.*

Garter Ceremony
St George's Chapel, Windsor Castle (2nd Mon). *Procession of Sovereign and Knights.*

Admiral of the Medway's Cruise
River Medway, Rochester (end of the month or early July, depending on the tides). *The mayor beats the bounds of the city then travels in a boat.*

JULY

Admiralty Court
Rochester Pier, The Esplanade (1st or 2nd Sat, depending on the tides). *The Mayor holds court in a barge.*

Black Cherry Fair
Windsor St, Chertsey (2nd Sat). *Parade of floats through town.*

Swan-Upping on the Thames
River Thames from Sunbury to Pangbourne, (3rd full week in Jul, Mon to Thu). *Marking of swans by boatmen in livery (see page 40).*

AUGUST

Mary Gibson's Legacy
St Nicholas's Church, Sutton (12th). *Preaching of sermon and distribution of alms.*

SEPTEMBER

Barnet Horse Fair
Barnet. *A week-long fair dating back 700 years.*

Clog and Apron Race
Royal Botanic Garden, Kew, London (end of the month). *Race between horticultural students.*

OCTOBER

Old Man's Day
Braughing, nr Stevenage (2nd). *Commemoration of Mathew Wall who came to life after seeming to die.*

DECEMBER

The Crookham Mummers' Play
Crookham Village, Aldershot (Boxing Day). *Traditional mummers' play.*

Atlas

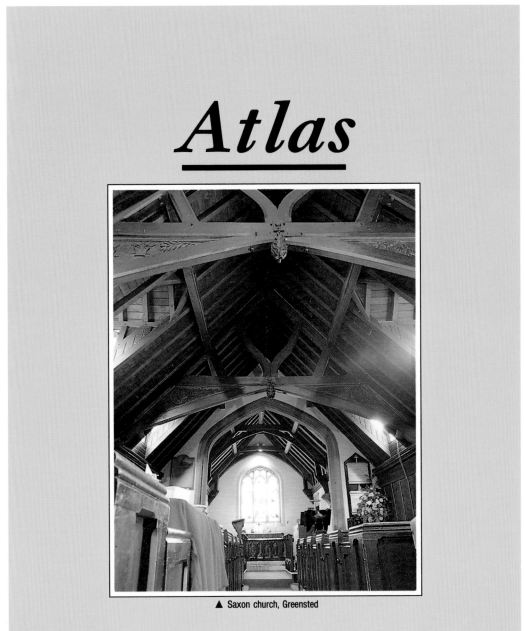

▲ Saxon church, Greensted

The following pages contain a legend, key
map and atlas of the countryside around
London, four circular motor tours and
sixteen planned walks to the north, south,
east and west of the capital.

MAP SYMBOLS

THE GRID SYSTEM

The map references used in this book are based on the Ordnance Survey National Grid, correct to within 1000 metres. They comprise two letters and four figures, and are preceded by the atlas page number.

Thus the reference for Harlow appears 89 TL 4611

89 is the atlas page number

TL identifies the major (100km) grid square concerned (see diag)

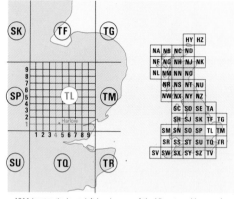

4611 locates the lower left-hand corner of the kilometre grid square in which Harlow appears.

Take the first figure of the reference 4, this refers to the numbered grid running along the bottom of the page.
Having found this line, the second figure 6, tells you the distance to move in tenths to the right of this line. A vertical line through this point is the first half of the reference.

The third figure 1, refers to the numbered grid lines on the right hand edge of the page, finally the fourth figure 1, indicates the distance to move above this line. A horizontal line drawn through this point to intersect with the first line gives the precise location of the places in question.

KEY TO ATLAS
1 : 300,000 – 1" TO 4.7 MILES
ATLAS 1 : 200,000 – 1" TO 3.15 MILES
ROADS AND RAILWAYS

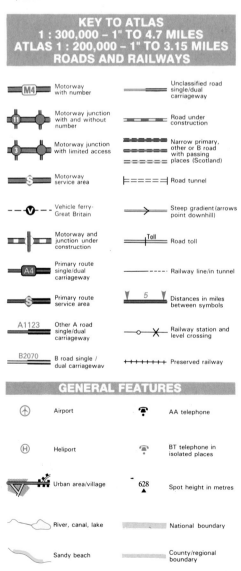

M4	Motorway with number		Unclassified road single/dual carriageway
11	Motorway junction with and without number		Road under construction
3	Motorway junction with limited access		Narrow primary, other or B road with passing places (Scotland)
S	Motorway service area		Road tunnel
V	Vehicle ferry-Great Britain		Steep gradient (arrows point downhill)
	Motorway and junction under construction	Toll	Road toll
A4	Primary route single/dual carriageway		Railway line/in tunnel
S	Primary route service area	5	Distances in miles between symbols
A1123	Other A road single/dual carriageway		Railway station and level crossing
B2070	B road single / dual carriageway	+++++	Preserved railway

GENERAL FEATURES

Airport		AA telephone	
Heliport		BT telephone in isolated places	
Urban area/village		628	Spot height in metres
River, canal, lake			National boundary
Sandy beach			County/regional boundary

TOURIST INFORMATION

Tourist Information Centre		Hill fort	
Tourist Information Centre (seasonal)		Roman antiquity	
Abbey, cathedral or priory		Prehistoric monument	
Ruined abbey, cathedral or priory		1066	Battle site with year
Castle		Preserved railway/steam centre	
Historic house		Cave	
Museum or art gallery		Windmill	
Industrial interest		Golf course	
Garden		County cricket ground	
Arboretum		Rugby Union national ground	
Country park		International athletics stadium	
Agricultural showground		Horse racing	
Theme park		Show jumping/equestrian circuit	
Zoo		Motor racing circuit	
Wildlife collection—mammals		Coastal launch site	
Wildlife collection—birds		Ski slope—natural	
Aquarium		Ski slope—artificial	
Nature reserve		NT	National Trust property
RSPB site		Other places of interest	
Nature trail		Boxed symbols indicate attractions in urban areas	
Forest drive		National Park (England & Wales)	
National trail		National Scenic Area (Scotland)	
AA viewpoint		Forest Park	
Picnic site		Heritage Coast	
		Blue flag beach	

TOURS

2	Start point of tour		Featured tour
	Direction of tour	6	Point of Interest

TOURIST INFORMATION

Camp Site		Nature reserve
Caravan Site		Other tourist feature
Information Centre		Preserved railway
Parking Facilities		Racecourse
Viewpoint		Wildlife park
Picnic site		Museum
Golf course or links		Nature or forest trail
Castle		Ancient monument
Cave		Places of interest
Country park		Telephones : public or motoring organisations
Garden		PC Public Convenience
Historic house		Youth Hostel

◆ ◆◆ ◆ Waymarked Path / Long Distance Path / Recreational Path

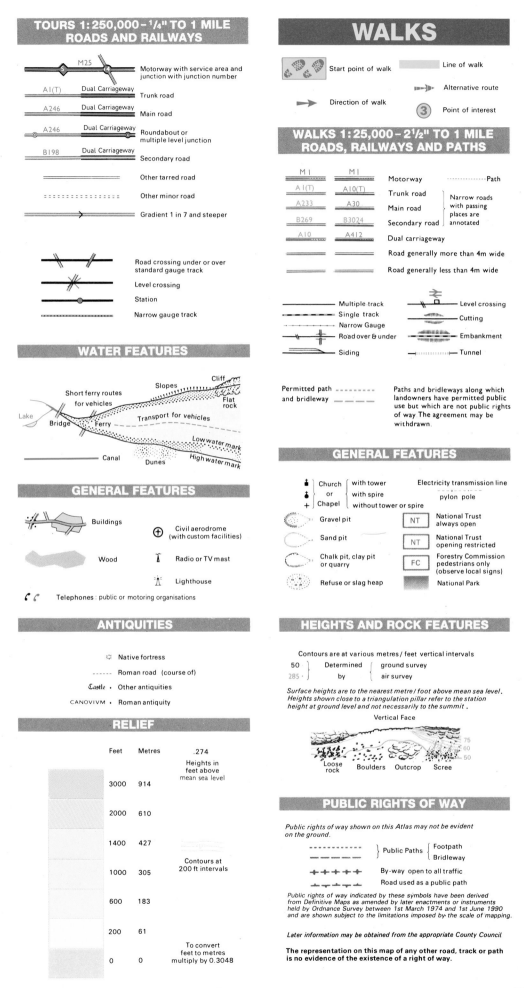

TOURS 1:250,000 – ¼" TO 1 MILE ROADS AND RAILWAYS

M25 — Motorway with service area and junction with junction number

A1(T) Dual Carriageway — Trunk road

A246 Dual Carriageway — Main road

A246 Dual Carriageway — Roundabout or multiple level junction

B198 Dual Carriageway — Secondary road

Other tarred road

Other minor road

Gradient 1 in 7 and steeper

Road crossing under or over standard gauge track

Level crossing

Station

Narrow gauge track

WATER FEATURES

Cliff
Slopes
Flat rock
Short ferry routes for vehicles
Lake
Bridge Ferry
Transport for vehicles
Low water mark
Canal
Dunes
High water mark

GENERAL FEATURES

Buildings

Wood

Telephones : public or motoring organisations

⊕ Civil aerodrome (with custom facilities)

Ï Radio or TV mast

Lighthouse

ANTIQUITIES

Native fortress

Roman road (course of)

Castle • Other antiquities

CANOVIVM • Roman antiquity

RELIEF

Feet	Metres	
		.274
		Heights in feet above mean sea level
3000	914	
2000	610	
1400	427	
1000	305	Contours at 200 ft intervals
600	183	
200	61	
0	0	To convert feet to metres multiply by 0.3048

WALKS

Start point of walk

Line of walk

Direction of walk

▶▶▶ Alternative route

③ Point of interest

WALKS 1:25,000 – 2½" TO 1 MILE ROADS, RAILWAYS AND PATHS

M1	M1	Motorway	.... Path
A1(T)	A10(T)	Trunk road	Narrow roads with passing places are annotated
A233	A30	Main road	
B269	B3024	Secondary road	
A10	A412	Dual carriageway	

Road generally more than 4m wide

Road generally less than 4m wide

Multiple track

Single track

Narrow Gauge

Road over & under

Siding

Level crossing

Cutting

Embankment

Tunnel

Permitted path and bridleway — Paths and bridleways along which landowners have permitted public use but which are not public rights of way. The agreement may be withdrawn.

GENERAL FEATURES

Church or Chapel { with tower / with spire / without tower or spire }

Gravel pit

Sand pit

Chalk pit, clay pit or quarry

Refuse or slag heap

Electricity transmission line

pylon pole

NT National Trust always open

NT National Trust opening restricted

FC Forestry Commission pedestrians only (observe local signs)

National Park

HEIGHTS AND ROCK FEATURES

Contours are at various metres / feet vertical intervals

50 } Determined { ground survey
285 · } by { air survey

Surface heights are to the nearest metre / foot above mean sea level. Heights shown close to a triangulation pillar refer to the station height at ground level and not necessarily to the summit.

Vertical Face

75
60
50

Loose rock Boulders Outcrop Scree

PUBLIC RIGHTS OF WAY

Public rights of way shown on this Atlas may not be evident on the ground.

------- } Public Paths { Footpath / Bridleway

+++++ By-way open to all traffic

Road used as a public path

Public rights of way indicated by these symbols have been derived from Definitive Maps as amended by later enactments or instruments held by Ordnance Survey between 1st March 1974 and 1st June 1990 and are shown subject to the limitations imposed by the scale of mapping.

Later information may be obtained from the appropriate County Council

The representation on this map of any other road, track or path is no evidence of the existence of a right of way.

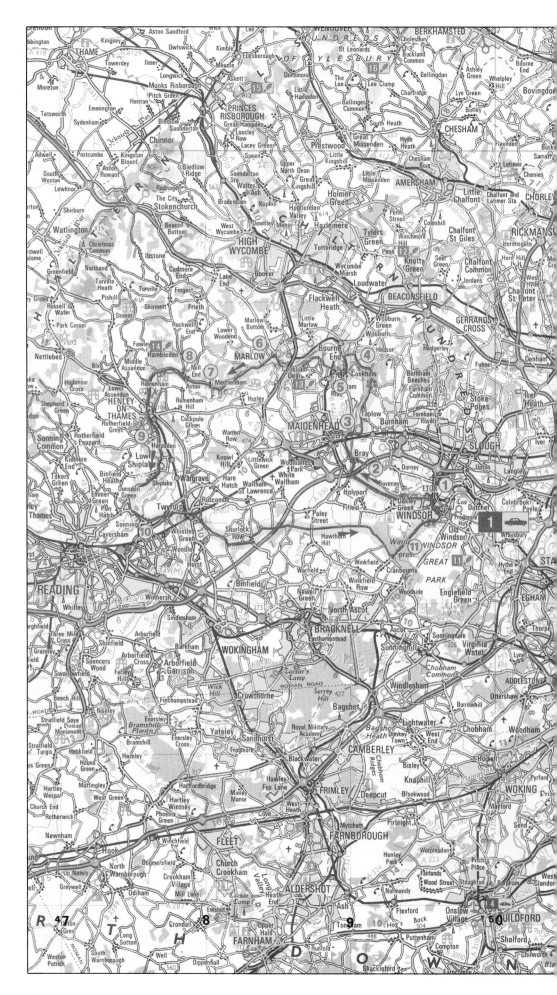

TOUR 1
REACHES OF THE THAMES

From the splendour of Windsor to the beautifully kept Thames-side villages set beneath beech woods and rolling hills, this gentle tour is packed with delightful places in which to stop and wander.

ROUTE DIRECTIONS

The drive starts from Windsor ①.
46 miles

Leave Windsor on the A308, signposted Maidenhead. In 4 miles pass under the motorway bridge and turn right on to the B3028 for Bray ②.

At the end of the village bear right, continue for 1 mile to the edge of Maidenhead, then turn left on to the A4, go right round the roundabout and double back to cross Maidenhead Bridge ③.

Continue on the A4 for nearly ½ mile, then turn left, signposted Taplow and Cliveden, up Berry Hill. Continue through Taplow, and in 2 miles pass the entrance to Cliveden on the left (see page 00). In just over ¼ mile turn left on to an unclassified road, signposted Bourne End. In about ½ mile pass Hedsor Priory to the right ④.

In ¼ mile turn left on to an unclassified road, signposted Cookham. In nearly ½ mile turn left on to the A4094, signposted Cookham, and later cross the Thames for Cookham ⑤.

Turn right into the main street by the Spencer Gallery. Cross Cookham Moor common and in ½ mile, before the White Hart Inn, turn right, signposted Winter Hill Golf Course. The lane winds uphill, eventually reaching the National Trust viewpoint of Winter Hill. The views from here stretch across to the Chilterns, with Marlow in the foreground.

In ¼ mile bear right and descend (10%) through beech woods with some sharp bends. At the next T-junction turn right and cross the Thames, into Marlow ⑥.

At the end of Marlow High Street turn left on to the A4155, signposted Henley, and continue to Medmenham ⑦. Continue through Mill End, passing the sign to Chilton Valley Winery and Brewery to the right ⑧.

Continue on the A4155 to Henley ⑨.

Leave Henley on the A4155, signposted Reading, and in 2 miles pass through Shiplake.

Just before the Flowing Spring pub turn left (one-way), signposted Sonning. At the end turn left again on to the B478 for Sonning ⑩.

Bear left through the village and at the roundabout on the A4 take the 2nd exit on to the A3032, signposted Twyford. In Twyford turn right on to the A321, signposted Wokingham. After crossing the railway bridge keep forward on to the B3018 and continue to Shurlock Row. Turn left on to an unclassified road, signposted Maidenhead, into the village and at the far end turn right on to the Hawthorn Hill road. Later pass over the M4 and go over two crossroads, signposted New Lodge.

After 4 miles turn left on to the B3022, signposted Windsor, then turn left again and shortly pass Windsor Safari Park and Seaworld ⑪ on the left. Continue back into Windsor.

POINTS OF INTEREST

① Windsor, most famous for its huge, sprawling castle, has much to offer the visitor. There are attractive new shopping arcades and complexes to wander through, trips up and down the Thames to enjoy, and the Great Park to explore. Just across the bridge at the bottom of the town is Eton, where the school and yet more individual shops beckon (see also pages 43 and 73).

② Bray has a fine bridge designed by Brunel. The village is an attractive mixture of timber-framed and Georgian houses. Simon Alwyn was the famous Vicar of Bray who kept changing his creed in order to retain his living.

③ Its proximity to London and lovely riverside scenery have made Maidenhead a very popular commuter town. Just upstream is the even more popular Boulter's Inn on Boulter's Lock Island.

④ As the road dips down a footpath leads off to the right up to Hedsor Priory. There are lovely views from here across beech woods, and Lord Boston's Folly, built in the 18th century, can be seen on the hill opposite.

⑤ Stanley Spencer and swan-upping are most usually associated with Cookham and the gallery containing some of the painter's work is well worth visiting. His *Last Supper* hangs in the Holy Trinity Church. Boats can be hired near the bridge (see also page 40).

⑥ Another Thames-side treasure, Marlow suffers slightly from its popularity but is nevertheless a charming, lively Georgian town with a wide main street – full of good shops – and footpaths by the river (see also page 60).

⑦ It is hard to imagine that the peaceful village of Medmenham was once the centre of scandalous goings on by the Hellfire Club (see page 71). The no-through road to the left just before the church leads past pretty houses of all sizes to the river and a lovely riverside footpath.

⑧ Chilton Valley Winery and Brewery can be found by following the signs for some 3 miles. Visitors are welcome in the shop, and tours can be arranged.

⑨ Interesting shops, numerous inns and restaurants, boating and riverside walks all contribute to the charm of Henley (see also page 52).

⑩ Sonning's old mill has been turned into a theatre restaurant, and the wooden buildings can be seen to the right of the road on the approach to the village. The river here is spanned by an 11-arch bridge.

⑪ Pioneer of the concept of Safari Parks, Windsor's is as popular as ever and has been brought up to date with hair-raising rides and imaginative adventure playgrounds (see also page 73).

TOUR 2
THROUGH RURAL ESSEX

The tour reaches charming villages with windmills, ancient guildhalls, duck ponds and tiny local museums after skirting the two great forests of Epping and Hatfield.

ROUTE DIRECTIONS

The drive starts from Epping ①.
64 miles

From Epping follow the B1393, signposted Harlow. In 4 miles, at the roundabout, take the 1st exit on to the A414. At the next two roundabouts take the 2nd exit. At the next roundabout take the 3rd exit on to the B183. Continue for 4½ miles to the A1060 at Hatfield Heath. Turn right and in 200yds turn left on to the B183, signposted Takeley. Continue to Hatfield Broad Oak ②.

In 1¼ miles turn left along an unclassified road (no sign) that runs past Hatfield Forest Country Park ③.

Continue to the A120 and turn right. At the traffic lights in Takeley turn left on to an unclassified road, signposted Elsenham. In 2 miles turn right, signposted Broxted. Continue for 2 miles to a T-junction in Broxted. Turn right and in ½ mile join the B1051 and continue forward for 2½ miles to Thaxted ④.

Half a mile after leaving Thaxted, at the Four Seasons Hotel, turn right on to the B1051 and continue to Great Sampford. Turn right on to the B1053 and continue for just over 3 miles to Finchingfield ⑤.

Turn right on to the B1057 to Great Bardfield ⑥.

Continue on, through Bran End, to a T-junction on the outskirts of Great Dunmow ⑦.

Turn left at the junction and continue through the town centre. At the mini-roundabout take the 2nd exit, signposted Chelmsford. In ¼ mile turn right on to the B184, signposted Ongar. Continue to Leaden Roding.

At the A1060 turn right and in 1 mile turn left on to the B184. Continue to a roundabout on the outskirts of Chipping Ongar and take the 2nd exit on to the A113. In almost a mile reach Chipping Ongar ⑧.

At a river bridge turn right on to an unclassified road, signposted Greensted. Pass the lane to Greensted church on the right ⑨.

Continue for 3 miles to the A414 and turn left. In 1 mile, at the Talbot roundabout, take the 1st exit on to the B181. Continue to the traffic lights at the junction with the B1393 on the outskirts of Epping and turn left to return to the town centre.

POINTS OF INTEREST

① Epping, with its long, broad High Street, has managed to retain the air of a country market town and former coaching stop. It gives its name to the 6,000-acre forest which offers today's traveller plenty of scope for walking and picnicking (see also page 42).

② Eighteenth-century almshouses and some fine Georgian buildings are to be found in the pretty village of Hatfield Broad Oak. The church was originally part of a Benedictine Priory.

③ Over 1,000 acres of ancient woodland open to the public for walking, fishing and bird-watching make up Hatfield Forest Country Park. It is a rare surviving example of medieval forest management based on pasture for cattle and deer, rabbit warrens, pollard oak trees and coppice woodland (see also page 51).

④ The almost perfect small town of Thaxted contains a magnificent church, a 15th-century guildhall – now housing a small museum of local bygones – standing on wooden pillars above what was once an open market, a fine early 19th-century windmill and many other attractive buildings. When the wool trade was at its height Thaxted was a busy market town and owes much of its prosperous air to this era.

⑤ Finchingfield is most people's ideal of an archetypal English village. It has everything; a fine old church that dominates the village, a 16th-century guildhall (also housing a museum), a windmill, a green with a duck pond, almshouses, inviting pubs and many thatched cottages.

⑥ A large, thriving village of considerable charm, Great Bardfield is a delightful mixture of vernacular architectural styles and includes a 14th-century medieval hall house, a windmill, a lock-up and a Victorian town hall. The church, which lies on the southern edge of the village, contains a fine screen. Near by, set above the River Pant, is a timber-framed plastered hall dating from the 17th century. Place House was built in 1564 by William Bendlowes, a local benefactor.

⑦ Yet another attractive small town with a duck pond and some interesting buildings, Great Dunmow is best known for the tradition of the Dunmow Flitch. A side of bacon (flitch) is awarded every four years to a married couple who can prove that they have lived in harmony for a year and a day and not repented of their marriage (see also page 41).

⑧ Chipping Ongar once had a fine motte-and-bailey castle built by Eustace of Boulogne in 1086 and enlarged by Richard de Lucy in 1154, but now only the moat and castle mound remain. The town's name comes from the 'chipping', or market, which grew up beneath the castle.

⑨ It is claimed that St Andrew's, in Greensted, is the oldest wooden church in the world (see also page 48).

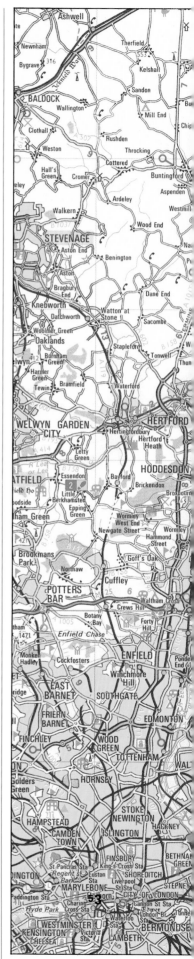

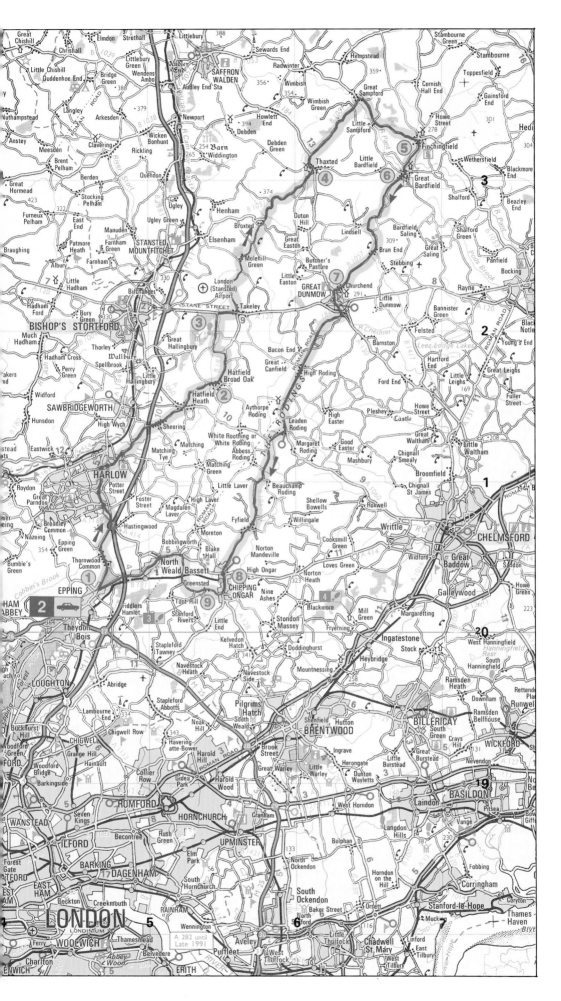

TOUR 3
ACROSS THE WEALD

Conical brick oast-houses with tilted caps, rows of apple and pear trees, hop-fields and bluebell woods are complemented by pretty villages and grand houses on this delightful tour in the heart of Kent.

ROUTE DIRECTIONS

The drive starts from Sevenoaks ①.
54 miles

From Sevenoaks follow the A2028 to leave by London Road and at the first roundabout take the 1st exit on to the A25, signposted Westerham. Shortly branch left on to the B2042. After about 3 miles pass the Churchill pub, then turn right, unclassified, signposted Emmetts Garden. Continue to Ide Hill ②.

At the roundabout in the village turn right. Shortly pass Emmetts Garden on the left ③.

At the crossroads immediately beyond Emmetts Garden, turn left, signposted Toys Hill. At the next T-junction turn left. There are lovely views of the Weald and Bough Beech Reservoir before the road descends (16%), passing Toys Hill on the right ④.

At the next crossroads turn right, signposted Puddledock, and on reaching the T-junction turn right again, signposted Westerham. In 1½ miles pass Chartwell on the right (see page 36).

In ½ mile, at the T-junction, turn left on to the B2026, signposted Crockham Hill. At the next T-junction turn left, signposted Edenbridge, to enter Crockham Hill. Opposite the Royal Oak in Crockham Hill turn left on to the B269, signposted Penshurst, and continue to Four Elms. Go over the crossroads on the B2027, signposted Tonbridge, B269, and in about 1½ miles bear right and turn left after the railway bridge, opposite the Wheatsheaf. Shortly turn right, unclassified, signposted Chiddingstone Castle. At the next crossroads turn left (the no-through road ahead leads to Chiddingstone Castle) ⑤.

Just past Chiddingstone village, opposite the oast-houses, branch left, signposted Chiddingstone Causeway. Cross the River Eden and at the T-junction turn right on to the B2027 to the village of Chiddingstone Causeway. At the church, turn right on to the B2176, signposted Penshurst. At the next T-junction turn right, and continue to Penshurst, passing Penshurst Place on the left (see page 61).

Turn right on to the B2188, signposted Tunbridge Wells, and continue to Fordcombe. In 1 mile, at the T-junction, turn right on to the B2110, signposted Groombridge. Descend, and at the Victoria pub branch left, unclassified, signposted Eridge, into Groombridge ⑥.

Pass Groombridge station, then bear left, signposted Tunbridge Wells. In 1½ miles branch left, signposted High Rocks ⑦.

Pass High Rocks Inn and continue forward, signposted Tunbridge Wells. At the next crossroads, turn right, signposted The Pantiles (see page 64).

At the next mini-roundabout turn left on to the A26, signposted Tunbridge, then branch right, signposted to the station. Cross the railway bridge and at the next mini-roundabout turn right on to the B2023 (no sign) into Grove Hill Road. Shortly bear left, signposted Hastings, B2023, and at the next traffic lights go forward. Shortly turn right on to the A264 (no sign), and in 1½ miles, at the next roundabout, go forward, signposted Hastings. At the following roundabout go forward on to the B2015, signposted Maidstone. Continue forward at the next traffic lights, and at the roundabout in 3¼ miles take the 2nd exit. The 1st exit leads into the Whitbread Hop Farm (see page 34).

Continue through East Peckham and in ½ mile branch left on to the B2016, signposted Wrotham Heath. Continue to the next roundabout and take the 2nd exit, signposted Wrotham. Shortly after, at the crossroads, turn left, signposted West Peckham. At West Peckham ⑧ bear right, signposted Plaxtol.

At the following crossroads go forward, signposted Crouch, and in just over a mile turn left, signposted Old Soar Manor. Pass Old Soar Manor on the right ⑨.

In ½ mile turn right, signposted Plaxtol. Shortly turn left and continue through Plaxtol ⑩.

At The Rorty Crankel pub in Plaxtol turn right, signposted Ightham, then at the church bear left. At the next T-junction turn right on to the A227, signposted Wrotham, then shortly turn left, signposted Ivy Hatch and Ightham Mote. Pass the road to Ightham Mote on the left (see page 55).

Continue to Ivy Hatch. After The Plough branch left, signposted Stone Street. By the Rose and Crown in Stone Street branch left, signposted Riverhill. Continue over the next crossroads and in 1½ miles, at the T-junction, turn right on to the A225 (no sign). Care required here.

Knole can be seen to the right on the approach to Sevenoaks, and the entrance to the estate is on the right in the town (see page 58).

POINTS OF INTEREST

① Sadly, six of the seven oaks that gave the town its name were blown down in 1987. Popular as a shopping centre, Sevenoaks has a pleasant main street, a cricket ground, a theatre, a swimming pool, a sports centre and a museum, plus the great house of Knole (see also page 65).

② Surrounding a sloping green, Ide Hill is a pretty little village with an attractive spired church. A path beside the church leads to an area owned by the National Trust from where there are some splendid views.

③ The charming shrub garden of Emmetts suffered severely during the 1987 hurricane (as did Ide Hill), but replacement replanting had already begun so this National Trust property has virtually been restored to its former glory. As one of the highest gardens in Kent, it has splendid views across the Weald.

④ The National Trust also owns land at Toys Hill where there is a wheelchair

route as well as several viewpoints. Octavia Hill, co-founder of the National Trust, made her home at nearby Crockham Hill and 100 acres of woodland here are named after her.

⑤ Gothicized in the early 19th century, Chiddingstone Castle belonged to the Streatfeild family whose mausoleum is in the churchyard in Chiddingstone village. A footpath leads from the village to the Chiding Stone, a large rock which stands on half an acre of land bequeathed to the National Trust by Lord Astor of Hever. It is said that tiresome, nagging wives were brought here, and then they in turn were nagged by the villagers who assembled for the fun.

⑥ Groombridge straddles the county border between Kent and East Sussex which is marked here by the Kent Water. Although it has grown in recent years, the old heart of the village is attractive with tile-hung houses and a green. Good rock-climbing can be found at Harrison's Rocks, to the south.

⑦ Rock-climbers are familiar with High Rocks as it is the headquarters of the Sandstone Climbing Club of Britain. Other interesting rock formations in the area include Toad Rock – named for obvious reasons – and Happy Valley.

⑧ The pleasant village of West Peckham has a delightful church named after St Dunstan. Inside, an intricately panelled raised family pew dominates the north chapel. Access to it used to be by a separate door to the outside.

⑨ Built by the Culpepper family, Old Soar Manor is a good example of a late 13th-century house. What remains is the solar, chapel, lavatorium and barrel-vaulted undercroft which features huge collar beams and king posts. The great hall was demolished and replaced with the present red-brick Georgian farmhouse.

⑩ Brick, tile and weatherboard predominate in the pretty village of Plaxtol. Its church was built in 1649, but all that has survived attacks by the Victorians and German bombing is the nave. There are some interesting wooden carvings here.

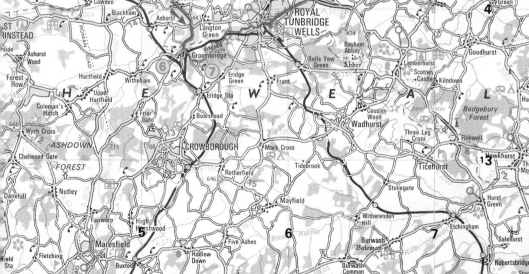

TOUR 4

THE SURREY HILLS

Surrey's wooded lanes and heathland predominate on this tour which has two great beauty spots – Frensham Ponds and the Devil's Punchbowl – as its highlights. In between lie peaceful, well-kept villages.

ROUTE DIRECTIONS

The drive starts from Guildford.
57 miles

Leave Guildford (see page 49) on the A3100, signposted Godalming. In just under a mile, opposite the Ships pub, turn right into Sandy Lane. Continue through the hamlet of Littleton and pass the entrance to Loseley House ①.

At the next T-junction turn right and continue to Compton (see page 39). Turn left at the junction at the end of the village and at the next roundabout take the 3rd exit, signposted Farnham. At the following roundabout take the 1st exit,

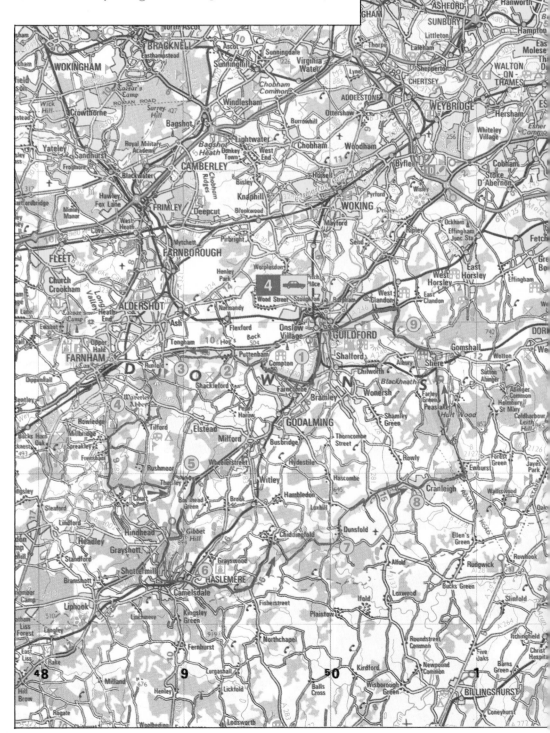

signposted Farnham. In 1 mile, just past The Jolly Farmer, turn left, signposted Puttenham ②.

Pass Puttenham church and keep forward, signposted Seale, and at the post office bear right. Continue on beneath the Hog's Back to Seale, pass Seale church on the right and at the end of the village turn left (no sign). Turn right here for Manor Farm Craft Centre ③.

At the next crossroads turn left, signposted Tilford. Continue over the following crossroads, and in ½ mile turn left at the T-junction on to Crooksbury Road. At the next T-junction turn left, signposted Tilford, then take the next turning right, signposted Tilford. In 1 mile cross a narrow (weak) bridge into Tilford (see page 67).

Go forward past the green and turn right at the T-junction, signposted Frensham, over another bridge. Shortly turn left, signposted Frensham. Pass the Rural Life Centre on the right ④.

In 1 mile turn left, signposted Hindhead. Before long Frensham Country Park (see page 44) is signposted to the right. Continue past Frensham Great Pond and in 1 mile, on a sharp bend, turn left, signposted Thursley. Continue to The Pride of The Valley Hotel and branch left over the crossroads, signposted Thursley. In just under 2 miles turn right to Thursley ⑤.

Keep forward, signposted Milford, and in ½ mile bear left, signposted Petersfield. Shortly turn right on to the A3, signposted Petersfield. Continue for 4½ miles to Hindhead, following the rim of the Devil's Punchbowl for some of the way.

At the traffic lights turn left on to the A287, signposted Haslemere. In 2 miles keep forward on the B2131. Continue through Haslemere ⑥.

After passing Haslemere station, keep a sharp look-out for signs to Petworth (A283). Turn left on to the A283, signposted Guildford. Continue to Chiddingfold. At the Crown pub turn right, signposted Dunsfold, and at the far side of the green turn right again. In 1 mile turn left, signposted Dunsfold. Continue on this road for about 4 miles to the village of Dunsfold ⑦.

In another mile, at the T-junction, turn right on to the B2130, signposted Cranleigh. In 1½ miles bear right, signposted Cranleigh, then turn right then left over the A281, signposted Cranleigh. At the next mini-roundabout turn right on to the B2128, signposted Horsham. Continue through Cranleigh ⑧.

At the mini-roundabout by the war memorial in Cranleigh turn left on to the B2127, signposted Ewhurst. In 2 miles keep left, signposted Ockley, to Ewhurst. In Ewhurst, at the Bulls Head, branch left, signposted Shere. The road climbs and eventually reaches Shere (see page 65). Continue through the village and at the T-junction turn left, signposted Guildford. Shortly turn left on to the A25. Pass the Silent Pool Car park on the right (see page 32). Continue up to Newlands Corner ⑨.

At the next traffic lights turn left, signposted Guildford (turn right then immediately left for Clandon Park, see page 38). In 1 mile, at the roundabout, take the 2nd exit, signposted Guildford. At the next lights keep forward (A3), signposted Guildford Centre.

POINTS OF INTEREST

① One thousand acres of farmland surround 16th-century Loseley House. Much of the stone used to build it was taken from Waverley Abbey whose ruins stand between Farnham and Elstead. There is much of interest in the house, including some good tapestries, and there are tractor rides around the farm that produces the famous range of Loseley Park ice cream, yoghurt and cheese from Jersey herds.

② Puttenham is a pleasant street village with cottages built of chalk, sandstone and redbrick. Among its buildings is Hurlands, the last country house built by Philip Webb. Puttenham Common, to the south-west of the village, is managed by Surrey County Council as an open space. It consists of 470 acres of sandy heathland and woodland and includes a chain of lakes.

③ Manor Farm Craft Centre is a small complex of craft workshops selling hand-made goods of high quality. There is also a restaurant here.

④ Old farm implements and machinery, together with exhibitions of agricultural crafts and trades, are displayed in the Old Kiln, farm buildings and surrounding woodland at the Rural Life Craft Centre.

⑤ Thursley's most outstanding feature is its common, now a National Nature Reserve where, among other things, the rare Dartford warbler may be found. The Reserve is exceptional in that it has one of the most extensive areas of bog to be found in this part of the country, and as a result there are many species of dragonfly here. The village itself has some pretty houses, and a nice pub, although there is no centre as such.

⑥ Another co-founder of the National Trust, Sir Robert Hunter, lived in Haslemere so it seems fitting that the town is surrounded by beautiful countryside, much of which is owned by the Trust. Based on a T-plan, Haslemere sprawls over a large area and is a pleasant mixture of good buildings, shops and markets. There is an Educational Museum in the High Street which covers geology, zoology, archaeology and history, plus peasant arts from Scandinavia and northern Europe.

⑦ The large common alongside which Dunsfold is built gives the village a rather more unkempt and remote feel than most of Surrey's other well-tended settlements. Near by is an airfield used for testing jets, and an oil well, but these do not impinge on Dunsfold's informal charm and the church is worth looking at.

⑧ Cranleigh is a pleasant enough small town with plenty of shops and a spreading residential area – despite the closing of its railway. The Cottage Hospital is claimed to be the first village hospital to be opened in England.

⑨ Newlands Corner is a well-known picnic and walking area. There is a large car park with footpaths leading to Albury, Chilworth, Guildford and West Clandon. Wonderful views take in the isolated St Martha's Church standing on top of the neighbouring wooded hill.

101

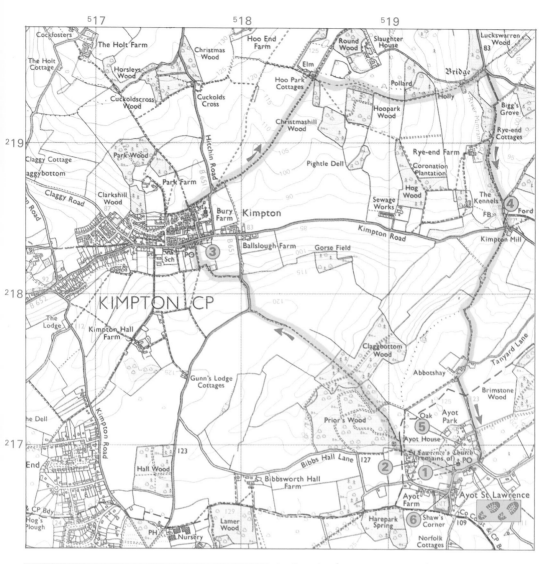

WALK 1

AYOT ST LAWRENCE

A fairly level walk through fields and woods with extensive views over pleasant Hertfordshire countryside. Two attractive villages provide added interest, and a visit can be made to the former home of George Bernard Shaw.

ROUTE DIRECTIONS

5 miles. Allow 2½ hours.
Start from the Brocket Arms (grid ref: TL196168). Cars may be parked in the lane.

From the pub, walk past the ruined church ①, then turn right along a stony track beside a pair of white cottages and follow a path across the fields towards the new church ②. When level with the church, turn right over a stile and follow the left-hand headland, ignoring a stile in the corner of the field. At the far left-hand corner of the field, cross a stile and walk through woods to a field and on to the road.

Cross the road and immediately turn right down the headland to the bottom of the field, turn left, walk behind the cricket pavilion, and then turn right down a path into Kimpton ③.

Turn right at the main road, then left up Church Lane to bear left along a metalled path. Turn right at the end of the path and then turn right again to walk parallel to the access road to the sports field.

At the road, turn left for a few yards, then turn right and follow a metalled route to Hoo Park Cottages.

Opposite the cottages, turn right over a stile into a field and aim for the left-hand edge of the wood ahead. Continue in the same direction through several fields and then drop down to a gate that gives access to a farm lane. Cross an old bridge, walk to the road and turn right.

Almost immediately, turn right along a track and then follow a lane to a T-junction ④. Turn right for a few yards and then turn left along a footpath, signposted Ayot St Lawrence. Turn right along a track between two large houses, then turn left soon after passing the entrance to Abbotshay Farm along a track that passes the Manor House and Ayot House ⑤ before returning to Ayot St Lawrence. Continue along the lane, past the Brocket Arms, to visit Shaw's Corner ⑥.

POINTS OF INTEREST

① The old parish church is a romantic ruin because, in 1770, Sir Lionel Lyle, the Lord of the Manor, attempted to demolish it because it spoilt his view.
② Sir Lionel built the extraordinary new church to enhance his park and, modelled on the Temple of Apollo at Delos, it is a rare example of a village church in the classical style.
③ Kimpton is a delightful village with buildings dating from the 16th century onwards. The large flint church with 13th-century wall paintings is worth visiting.
④ Note the watercress beds on the right.
⑤ The Manor House is a Tudor building with a late 17th-century front; Ayot House dates from the 18th century.
⑥ Shaw's Corner, now in the care of the National Trust, was the home of George Bernard Shaw from 1906 until his death in 1950. It remains exactly as he left it and contains many of his personal effects.

WALK 2

ESSENDON

An easy walk on well-defined paths through unexpectedly rural countryside lying just outside the M25. There are extensive views over Welwyn Garden City and the Lea valley. The route runs close to Hatfield House so the walk can be combined with a visit to this splendid Jacobean mansion.

ROUTE DIRECTIONS

4 miles. Allow 2 hours.
Start from the lay-by near the cricket field on the B158 (grid ref: TL275085).

From the footpath sign on the B158, walk along the edge of the cricket field then drop down through woods, ignoring all paths that diverge from the main route, and cross the footbridge over the Essendon Brook. Continue in the same direction through a kissing-gate and walk up a field, keeping the hedge on your right, to a stile at the top.

Turn left along a cross-track and after a few yards turn right at a footpath sign. In 55yds cross a stile and turn right to keep the hedge on your right. Continue in the same direction until reaching a road junction at the Candlestick public house.

Follow the lane with the No Through Road sign until reaching the end of the public highway (indicated by a gate across the road and a Private notice). Turn right and follow a wide stony track to Hillend Cottages where the route becomes metalled ① and ②. The metalled route turns sharp left on reaching the River Lea, at which point turn right and follow a track along the river ③.

Cross a field and turn right along a broad track enclosed with hedges. Turn left at a waymarked gap in the hedge, just after passing a farm track on the right. Cross two fields to reach the edge of a wood ④. Keep the wood on your left, follow the waymarks to the lane, then turn left to return to Essendon ⑤.

POINTS OF INTEREST

① On the left is the Home Park which forms part of the grounds of Hatfield House. The future Queen Elizabeth was confined in the old Hatfield Palace during Queen Mary's reign and hunted over the country through which this walk runs.
② Welwyn Garden City, visible across the valley, was built by the much admired Garden City movement after World War I and became a New Town in 1948.
③ In the 18th century, the River Lea was made navigable between Ware and London and became an important trade route for transporting malt and grain. Now the river is used for angling and boating.
④ The handsome early 19th-century stuccoed mansion visible on the hillside from here is Essendon Place.
⑤ Essendon church has been much restored and the chancel was wrecked by a bomb dropped from a Zeppelin in 1916. It contains a handsome black Wedgwood font given in 1778 by Mary Whitbread of the brewing family. Beatrix Potter often worshipped here when visiting her grandparents, who resided in Essendon.

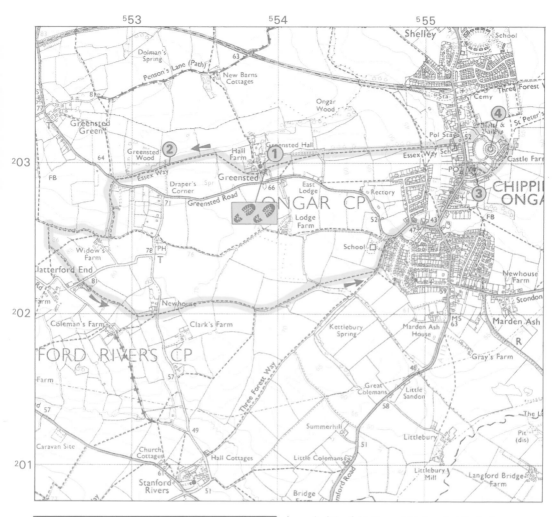

WALK 3

GREENSTED-JUXTA-ONGAR

Fields, woods, one of the oldest churches in England and the ruins of a motte-and-bailey castle feature on this walk. Ongar is an Anglo Saxon word meaning 'grazing land', and the description still holds true today.

ROUTE DIRECTIONS

4½ miles. Allow 2 hours.
Start from the car park near Greensted church (grid ref: TL539029).

From the car park, walk towards the church and turn left at a footpath sign ①. Follow the headland past a house, then strike diagonally right across the field ② and follow a stream to a road.

Cross over the road and follow the field edge beside a wood, then turn left over a stile about halfway along the field. Almost immediately, bear right in front of a stable and walk uphill through several small paddocks to a cross-track. Turn right, follow the waymarked route, keeping farm buildings on your left, and enter a huge field. Continue along the right-hand headland for 330yds and then turn left along a path that runs to the end of a hedge. Follow the right-hand side of this hedge to the lane at Clatterford End.

Turn left along the lane and then right at a footpath sign on the far side of the last cottage and walk alongside the garden. Enter the next field and immediately turn left and follow the hedge to the far

end of the field. Turn right, keeping the hedge on your left, and continue to the bottom of the field and enter the next field. Turn left over a stile and walk to a lane.

Cross over the lane and follow the path that runs in a straight line, through two small enclosures, to a gate. Continue in the same direction following the left-hand headland to the far end of the field. Pass through a gap in the hedge and then follow the right-hand headland of the next two fields. Pass through another gap and take the well-defined path that crosses the field diagonally, following the line of some utility poles. On reaching a broad track, turn left and walk to a road.

Turn right along the road and walk to a T-junction, turn left and walk into Chipping Ongar. Turn right at the jewellers, pass the church ③ and then take the signposted permissive path that encircles the motte-and-bailey castle ④ and return to the High Street. Cross the road and walk down Bansons Lane. This later becomes a track and continues as a path to emerge at Greensted.

POINTS OF INTEREST

① St Andrew's is famous for its wooden nave with timbers some 1,100 years old. Later additions include a Tudor chancel and a medieval weatherboarded tower with a shingled spire.
② This stretch forms part of the Essex Way, a route across Essex from Epping to Dedham through rolling, open country.
③ Chipping Ongar's church, with the unusual dedication to St Martin of Tours, is mainly Norman with some later additions.
④ All that now remains of the town's castle – its most significant Norman relic – is the castle mound to the north-east of the church. Traces of the moat can also be discerned. The wide High Street has some pleasant buildings, one of the oldest being the timber-framed jewellers.

WALK 4

MILL GREEN

From the quiet hamlet of Mill Green the walk crosses open fields and weaves in and out of typical Essex woodland. The beginning of the route picks up St Peter's Way.

ROUTE DIRECTIONS

6 miles. Allow 3 hours.
Start from the car park on Millgreen Common (grid ref: TL638012).

From the car park, walk across the common ① to a lane ②. Continue in the same direction to a junction, fork left, and follow a rough lane that becomes a track running through woods to reach a road.

Cross over the road and follow a concrete drive for 440yds, then turn right along a path that runs just inside a wood to a road. Cross over and follow the metalled bridleway past Barrow Farm. Just before the track becomes surfaced again, turn left over a stile and walk to the top of the field, aiming for a culvert between a utility pole and the tallest tree in the hedge. The path curves to the right across the next field and meets a road.

Turn right along the road for a few yards then turn left at a gap by a footpath sign and cross the field towards a line of poplar trees. A third of the way across the field, fork left. Cross a stile and turn left along a track that soon becomes metalled and joins a road.

Cross over the road and continue in the same direction, enter a field and follow the headland to the end. Turn right between some farm buildings and continue to a ditch and culvert. Do not cross the culvert but keep the ditch and intermittent hedge on the left. Bear right just beyond a utility pole and follow the waymarked route, keeping the hedge and ditch on your left, to a path that runs between houses to a road.

Cross the road to a footpath sign, walk up the driveway of the house and then continue between the houses to enter a field. Turn left and follow the headland until the hedge on the left turns sharp left. Bear right and aim for the left side of a clump of trees hiding a moat ③. Immediately beyond the moat, turn right over a footbridge and continue straight ahead to go downhill on the left-hand side of a ditch and hedge ④. Enter a wood and continue to a lane.

Turn left at the lane, enter a field and follow the headland, keeping the wood on your left, for 550yds, then turn sharp right and walk to the road.

Turn right and walk along the road, then turn left at a bridleway sign and walk to a wood. Turn left just inside the wood and continue in a straight line, ignoring paths that cross, to a road. Turn right to reach the car park.

POINTS OF INTEREST

① Mill Green is situated on a common (spelt Millgreen) and has a pub, a few 19th-century cottages and some larger, more modern houses. The windmill that can be glimpsed from the road is a privately owned post mill that gave its name to the hamlet.
② For about a mile the lane follows St Peter's Way, a path running 45 miles from Chipping Ongar to Bradwell-on-Sea. Most of the route follows fields and open tracks, with some marshland stretches.
③ Moats were sometimes built round larger houses in Essex, but they have no obvious purpose and appear to be little more than status symbols.
④ At this point the route crosses the grounds of Writtle Park, a Georgian house that lies to the east.

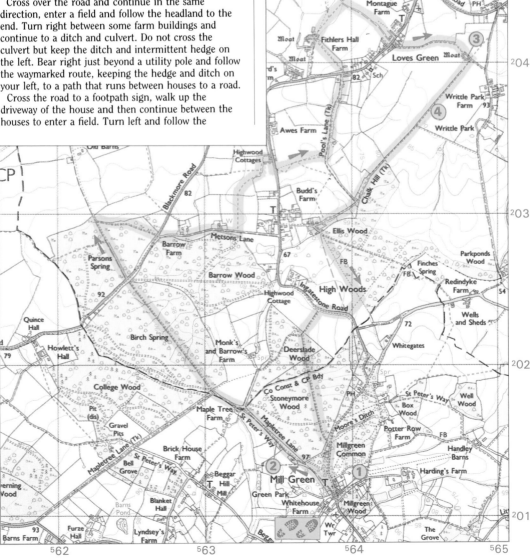

WALK 5
HIGHAM MARSHES

Old Higham lies at the end of a quiet lane just above the Thames estuary floodplain. Beyond the hamlet, the road continues as a footpath across the marshes to the tidal river which remains a busy waterway for large ships calling at Tilbury Docks upstream on the Essex shore.

ROUTE DIRECTIONS

4 miles. Allow 2½ hours (including church visit and diversion to fort).
Start from St Mary's Church, where there is parking by the churchyard wall beyond the lych-gate (grid ref: TQ716743).

Go through the gate at the end of the road by the church ① and follow the track past the farm buildings ② and over the level-crossing. Use the right-hand gate and then bear left across the field to the far corner.

Rather than be tempted over the wooden bridge, go through the gate in the corner where a notice warns 'penalty for not shutting the gate £2'. Climb over a stile and keep on the path running between drainage channels. At the far end go up the steep bank in front to continue northwards to the River Thames. Where the flood defence turns westwards, go down to the corner of the bay where there are two waymark stones – one for the Saxon Shore Way (SSW) ③.

Those who wish to see the fort ④ should continue north on the Saxon Shore Way. The main route is to the west along the shore, also part of the SSW.

Before reaching the prominent red beacon turn inland at the next SSW stone. Go down the high flood bank to

find a gate and stile. Follow the track south over Higham Marshes ⑤. Halfway across there is another gate just before the path passes the low Barrow Hill burial mound.

Where the path turns right to a gate go over the stile and at once cross over the footbridge. Keep ahead over a field to cross the railway line. The route bears left and runs into Higham by way of a farmyard and an easily missed pub ⑥.

POINTS OF INTEREST

① The ragstone church with its short, shingle spire has been a landmark for shipping from Saxon times. St Mary's is unusual in having a double nave. The original retains its screen, beyond which is a pre-Reformation aumbry to the right and an inscription to one of Henry VIII's Yeoman of the Guard to the left.
② Abbey Farm is on the site of the Benedictine Abbey Priory convent founded in 1148 with 16 sisters, but closed in 1521 when the number had fallen to three.
③ The Saxon Shore Way is a 140-mile path running from Gravesend to Rye tracing the old shoreline – for example Margate is bypassed as this is on the Isle of Thanet which was surrounded by water until the 16th century. The trail is waymarked with a red-horned helmet symbol.
④ Cliffe Fort was built between 1866 and 1871, along with Shornmead Fort to the west and Coalhouse Fort on the Essex bank opposite, to create a triangle of fire against an enemy sailing upstream to London.
⑤ The footpath inland across Higham Marshes largely follows the old ferry path to the village. A ferry from Coalhouse Point was operated by the Romans and continued until the mid 19th century.
⑥ The Sun is one of the least spoilt inns in Kent and does not even display its name, let alone a sign. It can be found just beyond the Old Vicarage and Clerk's Cottage – also unspoilt.

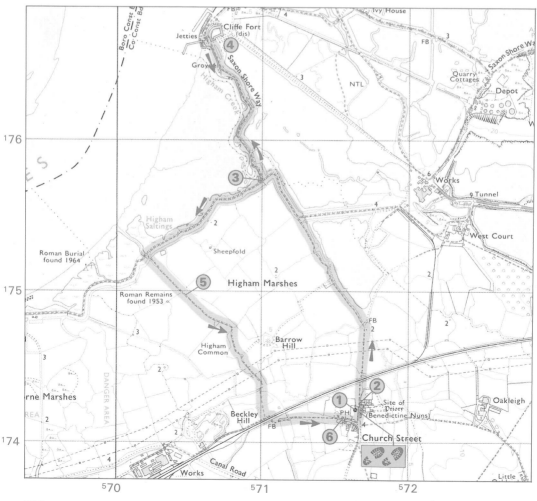

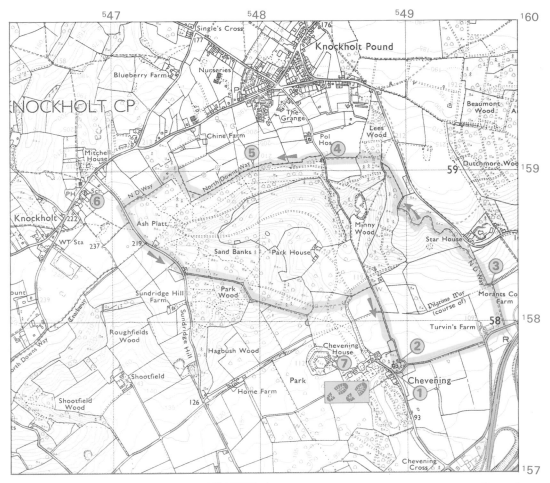

WALK 6

CHEVENING

Premier Lord Rosebury called Chevening 'Paradise' and Kipling was 'enchanted' while Arthur Mee declared that 'Kent has no lovelier corner so near to London'. A fine network of footpaths provides spectacular views across the Holmesdale valley.

ROUTE DIRECTIONS

4 miles. Allow 1½ hours.
Start from Chevening church (grid ref: TQ489577).

From the main street ① walk through the lych-gate to the church ②. Leave the churchyard at the far end, by the cross, to follow the green lane ahead. Continue as far as the road.

Go left along the road and just beyond the farm go over a stile on the left to join the North Downs Way. Where the path turns at a field corner it follows the Pilgrims' Way ③ for a few yards. Go right up through the trees to follow the side of the field up the hill. At the top, where there is a gap in the wood, go over a stile and keep to the left. The field soon opens out.

On reaching a drinking trough climb over the stile and follow the short, wide path through the wood. Go left to another stile and right along a field boundary to Chevening Lane ④. Turn right for a few yards to find a stile on the other side. Count each stile from here and at the fourth stand on top to look left down The Keyhole ⑤. After the path bears right there is a stile on the left leading to a wide path which narrows and bends. After another stile turn left up the side of a field to a lane at Knockholt ⑥.

Turn left along the lane and at Keeper's Cottage go left to walk up a wide woodland track. The way later bears half right down to a viewpoint. Continue down the path and over stiles to the kissing-gate. Walk round the corner and go over a stile to walk in front of the mansion ⑦. Switch to the other side of the fence at the drive. After another estate road go across a field to meet an enclosed track. Turn right to reach Chevening church.

POINTS OF INTEREST

① Chevening is at the crossroads of the old London road and the Pilgrims' Way which were diverted in 1792, leaving the mansion and village forgotten at the end of a lane. This is how novelist Jane Austen found Chevening, her 'Rosings Park', when visiting her brother who was the Rector.
② The building dates from the 13th century and its dedication to St Botolph, associated with travellers, recalls the Pilgrims' Way. The reredos is a stone reproduction of Leonardo da Vinci's *Last Supper* fresco in Milan.
③ The North Downs Way was opened in 1978 as the scenic successor to the Pilgrims' Way. This track takes its name from the pilgrims who passed along it from Winchester to St Thomas à Becket's shrine at Canterbury, although the trail is known to be pre-Roman.
④ This is the old London road. To the north is Ash Grove where Turner visited fellow artist William Wells in 1800 and produced a painting of the kitchen.
⑤ The tunnel of trees allowing a view of Chevening House is known as The Keyhole.
⑥ Knockholt is Kent's highest village. The church, dating from 1281, has a Susanna Thrale memorial window.
⑦ The mansion was designed by Inigo Jones in 1630 and the wings added in 1740 for the 1st Lord Stanhope. His family lived here for 250 years until 1967. The last Earl left Chevening to the nation in the hope that the Prince of Wales would make it his home. Prince Charles did so briefly until his marriage, and now the estate has become the Foreign Secretary's country residence.

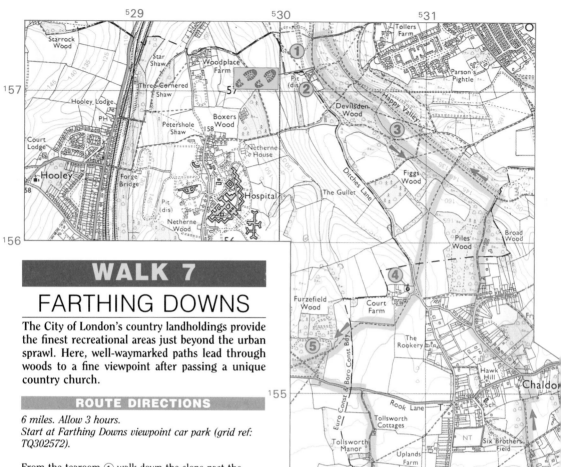

WALK 7
FARTHING DOWNS

The City of London's country landholdings provide the finest recreational areas just beyond the urban sprawl. Here, well-waymarked paths lead through woods to a fine viewpoint after passing a unique country church.

ROUTE DIRECTIONS

6 miles. Allow 3 hours.
Start at Farthing Downs viewpoint car park (grid ref: TQ302572).

From the tearoom ① walk down the slope past the information board to find the Downlands Circular Walk ② starting on a wide woodland path at the side of the buildings. Follow the path and bear left at a fork. The path runs out of the trees and along the side of Happy valley ③.

At the end of a second field, where there is a seat, turn into the wood and go over a stile. The path leads across a field and soon Chaldon church spire can be seen ahead. On the far side go left along a road for a few yards and then take the right turning to reach the church ④.

Just beyond the church go left over a stile to cut across the corner of a field to another stile. Turn right down the side of the field. Just before the bottom, the path cuts the corner to a stile. Continue in the same direction to run along the side of Furzefield Wood for a few yards before entering the trees.

Go ahead at a path junction to continue on a concrete path ⑤. At another junction turn left to reach Rook Lane. Turn left along the road for 300yds, passing Cold Blow Cottage, to the entrance of Tollsworth Manor.

Follow the manor driveway and at the farm turn left into a field. Go right with the track to reach a viewpoint ⑥. Turn left to join the North Downs Way which runs along an ancient hedged track.

Go ahead at Hilltop Lane. There are now trackside residences. After passing one with a clock, the path runs through a wood and continues downhill. Turn left here on to a narrow path with a set-back stile. The enclosed path runs ahead to a five-way path junction. Go ahead over the stile along the edge of a wood. After another stile the path is fenced as it follows two sides of a field to Rook Farm. Go straight over the road into Doctors Lane. At the post box turn right into Leazes Avenue. Keep to the left at a fork and go straight on to a woodland track running ahead.

On reaching a valley turn left to walk along the floor of Happy valley. Later the way narrows. Just before the horse track moves on to the main path, turn left. There is a wide steep slope ahead but take the path half-right up through the trees. On meeting a bridleway go left up on to the top of Farthing Downs.

POINTS OF INTEREST

① The chalk downland is part of the Coulsdon Commons acquired by the City of London Corporation in 1883 for the enjoyment of Londoners, along with Burnham Beeches and Epping Forest. The policy of saving London's countryside from developers continues and in 1991 the City purchased nearby Ashstead Common. From Farthing Downs there is a view of the new Canary Wharf tower in Docklands.

② This waymarked circular route was inaugurated in 1989 by the Lord Mayor of London who arrived in a cart drawn by two horses normally seen pulling his golden coach. The trail is designed to improve access to London's finest downland woods.

③ The 250-acre chalk valley, one of the few free of building, was saved from development in 1937. Its highly prized hay crop is fed to the local horses.

④ The medieval church, a few yards outside the boundary of Greater London, dates back to the 7th century. Its outstanding feature is a 12th-century mural painted by a travelling monk. Full of detail for use as a teaching aid, the unusual 17ft-high picture features a dishonest milkman and a drunken pilgrim. There is a pilgrim mark on the pillar by the door carved by a traveller who stopped off from the nearby Pilgrims' Way. On the east side of the churchyard there is the grave of Malcolm Campbell, who broke the land speed record.

⑤ The concrete paths were laid during World War II when this was used as a secret food store for use in the event of the capital being invaded.

⑥ The main view is of Redhill, but to the north it is sometimes possible to see the City's NatWest Tower.

WALK 8

BOX HILL

The Home Counties' steepest hills are around Box Hill, which has long been a place of recreation for Londoners who come for the panoramic views. Another tradition is the tearoom at the top which now has running water rather than the buckets brought up from the river below.

ROUTE DIRECTIONS

4½ miles. Allow 3 hours.
Start from the car park opposite the Burford Bridge Hotel (grid ref: TQ172520).

Walk past the Burford Bridge Hotel ① and continue on to the dual carriageway. After 600yds go left at a signpost to join the North Downs Way. Go over the river on the stepping stones ②. (If the stones are under water walk downstream to find a footbridge.)

Walk ahead on the path occasionally waymarked with the National Trust acorn symbol. The path is stepped as it rises steeply up the wooded hillside. At the top turn right to reach the Box Hill viewpoint ③.

On turning away from the view go half-left on to a path which joins the road before reaching the National Trust information centre and café. Once past the building, cross the road to follow a waymarked bridleway into the car park. Go right and then left to a wide path; its entrance is blocked to cars by a large log.

After passing a green, bear left off the main track at a National Trust bridleway post. Stay on this path, ignoring any turning to the right, to reach Broadwood's Folly ④. Turn right on to a path which bends. At a junction go right with the waymark to reach steps leading down into Juniper Bottom. Turn left on to the valley path.

At the road go ahead up the very steep and only partly-stepped path. At the top the way bears right to a viewpoint seat. Beyond the seat turn sharp left and keep ahead. Soon the path runs downhill and across a bridleway ⑤. At a stile go ahead to Mickleham church ⑥.

Turn left along the road. Use the pavement on the right which soon becomes a footpath running below and then above the road. On rejoining the road keep forward to Burford Bridge.

POINTS OF INTEREST

① Lord Nelson and John Keats knew this hotel as The Fox & Hounds when they stayed here. Others who used this resting place on the London-to-Dorking road were Byron, Sheridan and Wordsworth. As a princess, Queen Victoria called in for tea. In the 1830s the inn was an hour by horse-drawn coach from the Elephant & Castle in south London.

② This is considered to be part of the Pilgrims' Way. The present set of stones was inaugurated by Prime Minister Clement Attlee in 1946. The River Mole rises in Crawley and joins the Thames at Hampton Court.

③ From here there is a view of Dorking and the South Downs 24 miles away. In 1914 the viewpoint was given to the National Trust which has extended its protection to over 1,000 acres.

④ The flint tower was erected in about 1815 by piano maker James Broadwood who lived at Juniper Hall, seen below. Since the look-out's doorway was blocked up a tree has grown inside.

⑤ The bridleway follows the line of the Roman Stane Street running from London to Chichester.

⑥ The slightly off-set east end is a 'weeping chancel' representing Christ's head on the cross. The font is Norman. Diarist Fanny Burney, who had just resigned as the Queen's Second Keeper of the Robes, married General D'Arblay here in 1793. Outside the porch is the tomb of Canadian Prime Minister Lord Bennett who lived near by at Juniper Hill.

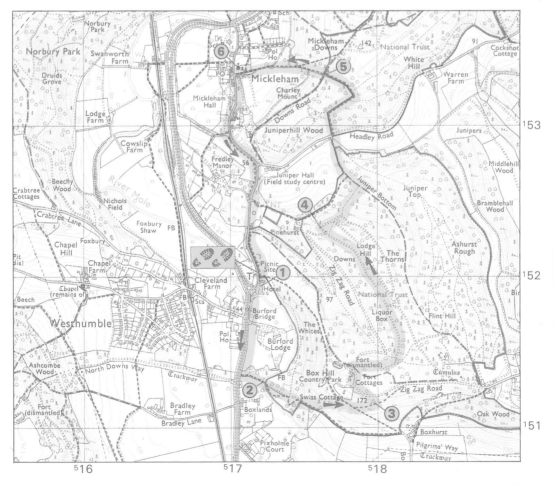

WALK 9
EPSOM DOWNS

On Derby Day there can be over 250,000 people on Epsom Downs but few ever see the place without the open-top buses, caravans and fun fair. London is visible from this high point where footpaths radiate out across to Walton Downs.

ROUTE DIRECTIONS

6 miles. Allow 3 hours.
Start from Tattenham Corner Road car park (grid ref: TQ224584).

Turn away from the stands ① to walk parallel with The Derby course ②. Keep by the road as it crosses the five-furlong start to bend round Tattenham Corner ③.

Once at The Mound, walk just inside the barrier. Soon there is a rough path which runs gently downhill to bear right with a gallop. Where the way is separated from the gallop and enjoys wide verges, look for an obscure entrance in the trees on the left.

A narrow path runs into the wood and at a junction, where there is a handy Downs map, continue ahead on a narrow path which climbs to follow a line of gardens. At a lane keep forward, past a left turn, up to a bend and take the steep footpath at the side of Derry. At a junction by a London boundary post turn right. Stay on the enclosed path until reaching a road at Pilgrims' Corner.

Turn left along the road and then right to walk down to a lay-by where a bridleway runs to Great Hurst Wood. Keep with the wood to go uphill and under the M25. About 100yds after the path enters trees, go over a stile on the right and up to a stile on the edge of the wood. Ahead is Headley church ④.

By the church kissing-gate go over a stile to an enclosed path. At a divide go right. Turn right at a lane to pass under the M25 again. At once go left on to a footpath. After a short distance go over a stile on the right to follow a path which is soon fenced. At the far end bear right to the road. Go right and left on to a wide wooded path. At the bottom turn left and bear half-right on to a rising wooded path. At a junction turn right into the open and across a gallop to go up the side of Walton Downs.

After running through the edge of a wood ⑤ the path meets the end of a wide track at a viewpoint. Continue just inside the barrier, but fork left where the path divides into a footpath and gallop. Turn right at a wide track which runs out of the wood and across Epsom Downs.

POINTS OF INTEREST

① There has been racing on the Downs since James I's reign. The attractive little Prince's Stand has survived since 1879, while the Grandstand has been rebuilt several times – most recently in 1991. As a child, Mrs Beeton, of Household Management fame, lived in the Grandstand due to her father being Clerk of the Course. The Rubbing House pub to the west of the stands was once a wooden building where horses were rubbed down between heats.

② The Derby, which takes place on the first Wednesday in June, was first run in 1780 after Lord Derby and Sir Thomas Bunbury tossed a coin to see which should give their name to the horse race. Describing the lunchtime scene, Charles Dickens wrote, 'All the hampers fly wide open and green Downs burst into a blossom of Lobster Salad'.

③ Tattenham Corner is the racecourse bend where suffragette Emily Davidson dashed in front of the King's horse in 1913. The discovery of a return train ticket in her pocket casts doubts on the suggested suicide.

④ The village appears in Domesday Book as Hallaga meaning 'clearing in the heather' and the current Headley spelling was only settled in 1899. The Victorian church replaces a 14th-century building, but the landmark tower by G E Street is built of materials from the old church which, as can be seen from the remains, stood to the south. Charles II's arms are in the new church.

⑤ The wood covers the grounds of Charles II's hunting lodge, built here to be near Epsom's spa where fashionable visitors included Samuel Pepys.

▼ Epsom racecourse

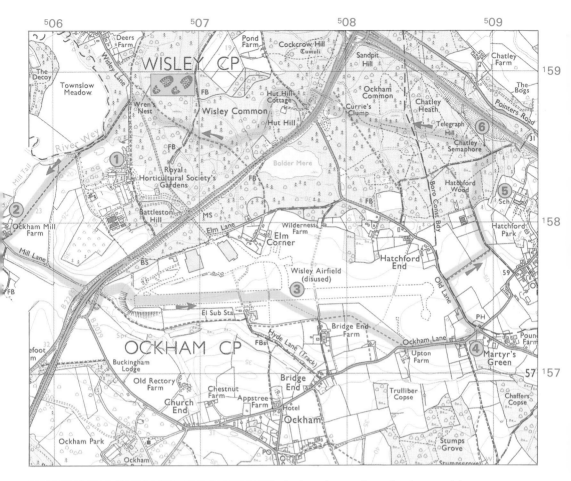

WALK 10

WISLEY

Wisley is the original garden centre, set in an extensive wood. Beyond its boundaries is the River Wey, a footpath which has reclaimed an airfield, and a pre-telephone government communication centre in another woodland setting.

ROUTE DIRECTIONS

5 miles. Allow 3 hours.
Start from Wren's Nest car park at the south end of Wisley village (grid ref: TQ066588).

Cross the road to walk up the Wisley Gardens' concrete exit driveway and turn right at the lodge to a stile. Follow the fenced footpath through the Gardens ①.

The path passes briefly alongside the River Wey and across a meadow to a stile. Keep in the same direction over a roadway. Soon the path is enclosed and meets a lane. Walkers may turn right here to look at the mill ②, but the main walk continues to the left along Mill Lane. At the end go over the slip road and through the tunnel under the A3 to cross another slip road. Turn left and just beyond a bus stop go right to a junction of footpaths.

Go over the stile and follow the path up the hill to another stile on the skyline. Follow the line of the public footpath running between yellow lines down a runway ③. After two sets of barriers, the lines lead off the airfield and across a field towards farm buildings.

Cross a track by the stiles to follow the side of a field. Go over two stiles and across the corner of a field to a stile at a road opposite Upton Farm. Turn left up to The Black Swan ④. Turn left and at the bottom of the hill go right over a stile. Keep by the fence and after three stiles the path meets a bridleway near a mansion ⑤.

Turn left at the path and at the bottom of the hill bear half-right on to a very wide bridleway running through a wood. At a barrier turn right up a narrow bridleway. On meeting a metalled path turn left to the tower ⑥.

Continue past the tower on to a wide path. Where it divides keep right, and then continue ahead in the same direction, ignoring all turnings, to reach a car park. Follow the path marked toilets and continue past the building to cross the bridge over the dual carriageway to wooded Wisley Common.

On the far side of the common turn left through a gateway and then follow a wooded track round to the right. After a short distance bear left on to a wide bridleway. Where the way divides keep left. As the bridleway turns left, continue ahead on a narrow path marked no horses. At the end turn right on to a wider path. After a four-way junction continue for 400yds to find Wrens' Nest car park through the trees on the left.

POINTS OF INTEREST

① Wisley's Royal Horticultural Garden was originally a 60-acre plot owned by the Society's Treasurer G F Wilson. Since the RHS took over in 1904, almost every style of garden has been laid out in the expanding grounds.
② The brick Ockham Mill, built in 1862 and now used as living accommodation, has unusual Norman-style doorways. There was a mill here in 1297.
③ The former airfield, part of World War II's defences, was used to test Hawker aircraft and although it appears operational there are barriers across the runway. The public footpath zigzags down the runway on its pre-War field route.
④ The rustic-fronted Black Swan pub is open all day, serving a wide range of beers and coffee.
⑤ Hatchford Park, a mansion dating from 1842, is now a school.
⑥ The 60ft tower was built in 1822 as one of 15 signal stations between the Admiralty and Portsmouth. Six words a minute could be transmitted by staff working in the first-floor operating room. Since then this heath viewpoint has been encroached by pine and birch.

111

▲ Virginia Water, covering about 160 acres

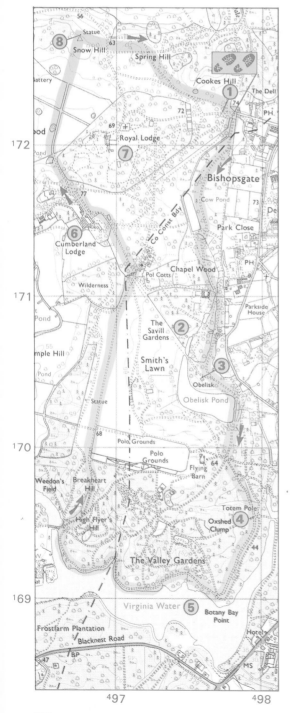

WINDSOR GREAT PARK

Lakes, fields, woods, valleys, hills and viewpoints which have for generations provided escape from central London for the Royal Family can be enjoyed by anyone so long as they are on foot. Cars must be left outside the gates.

ROUTE DIRECTIONS

6 miles. Allow 3 hours.
Start from Bishopsgate car park (grid ref: SU728973).

Go through Bishopsgate into Windsor Great Park ① and at once turn left along the side of the lodge to a green gate leading to the Rhododendron Ride. Where the path divides keep right.

On reaching a road keep straight on past the Savill Garden ②. Continue past the Obelisk ③ and Obelisk Pond. At a five-way junction go half-left on the metalled lane which leads to the totem pole ④.

Continue ahead where the way becomes rough. The path runs along the edge of Valley Gardens and parallel to Virginia Water ⑤.

At a large inlet, opposite a house, the path meets a road. Turn right along the road which later runs along the side of Smith's Lawn polo ground. Once through Cumberland Gate bear half-left off the road on to a footpath running through the trees and across two bridleways to join a wider path. Where this divides keep left.

Cross the drive to Cumberland Lodge ⑥ and after passing a tennis court go ahead to a junction of paths and roads. Keep forward to take the path half-right, opposite Chaplain's Lodge.

The gravel track runs downhill alongside the Royal Lodge garden fence to Ox Pond. Go ahead on the 'walkers only' wide grass path. Soon there is a view (right) across to the pink-washed Royal Lodge ⑦. Beyond the deer gate, go up to the Copper Horse viewpoint ⑧.

From the statue turn right to find a path running through the trees and over the rising grass. At the top the path joins the parallel road at a bend. Stay on the road and once through the deer gate go left along the side of a bridleway to Bishopsgate.

POINTS OF INTEREST

① William the Conqueror began the park and introduced the deer. George III personally supervised staking out the roads which remain free of through traffic.
② The Savill Garden is named after Sir Eric Savill who, encouraged by George V and Queen Mary, turned it into an all-seasons garden.
③ The Obelisk commemorates the Duke of Cumberland who put down the last Jacobite rebellion in 1746.
④ A single log from British Columbia was used to make this 100ft-high totem pole in 1958.
⑤ Virginia Water was dug to create work for the Duke of Cumberland's troops after the Battle of Culloden in 1746.
⑥ The mansion-size lodge, built by Charles II, was the Park Ranger's residence. Now much remodelled, it is used as a conference centre.
⑦ This has been the Queen Mother's country home since she was Duchess of York. Its pink wash was chosen as a reminder of her childhood home in Hertfordshire. Royal Lodge was the childhood home of The Queen and Princess Margaret.
⑧ Snow Hill, once called 'Snowdon', affords a spectacular view of Windsor Castle. The copper horse statue by Richard Westmacott depicts George III in Roman dress on a fine horse.

WALK 12

HODGEMOOR WOODS

From the Forestry Commission's Hodgemoor Woods – which offer plenty of walking in their own right – this route strikes off across farmland to the charming town of Amersham on the River Misbourne. On the way back there are good views.

ROUTE DIRECTIONS

6 miles. Allow 3 hours.
Start from the Hodgemoor Woods Forestry Commission car park just off the A355 (grid ref: SU960941).

Pass through a gap in the north-east corner of the car park and walk down the field-edge. Bear left at the bottom of the field, cross a stile on the right and walk to a stile at the bottom of the field. Follow a waymarked path through a series of fields and cross the A355 ①.

Follow a headland path to a cross-track. Turn right and follow the path to the road near Coleshill House ②.

Continue in the same direction along the road to where it turns sharp right. Bear left along a sunken path that emerges into a field, and then follow the right-hand headland to the bottom of the field. Cross the ditch on your right and immediately turn left to continue downhill to cross the footbridge over the bypass. Turn right, walk to the roundabout, and turn left.

At the T-junction, turn right (turn left here to visit Amersham ③). Shortly enter the yard of Bury Farm ④. Bear left through the farmyard and walk under the concrete viaduct. Continue for another 200yds, cross a stile on the right, walk uphill and enter Rodger's Wood. Continue into a field and after 220yds cross a farm track and continue in the same direction to meet a hedge that should be kept on the right.

Just before reaching Day's Wood, cross a stile on the right into a large field crossed by pylons. Pass to the left of the nearest pylon and continue to the stile in the hedge. Walk down the next field, keeping the hedge on your right, to a stile at the bottom, bear right and follow the field edge towards Upper Bottom House Farm. Just before reaching the farm, bear left and walk to a stile and a lane.

Turn right and then left along the track that climbs the hill opposite the farm and fork right at the wood. Shortly after passing Kiln Cottage, cross the stile on the right and walk to the next stile. Continue in the same direction through a large field, bearing slightly right just beyond Welpley's Wood, then keep to the bottom of a dry valley until reaching a lane.

Turn left for 220yds and then right at a footpath sign and stile and walk up the hill, keeping the hedge on your left. At the top of the field, cross the stile on the left and continue with the hedge on your right through a series of fields to a stile near Brentford Grange Farm. Retrace your steps to the car park.

POINTS OF INTEREST

① The windmill visible across the valley from this point is a tower mill built in 1856. It stands on the edge of Coleshill Common.

② Coleshill House was built to the north of the village of Coleshill in 1660, but the existing stuccoed front is Georgian.

③ The old town of Amersham has many delights, including the parish church, the 16th-century market hall and a number of welcome, and attractive, old inns.

④ Bury Farm was the home of Gulielma Springett who became the first wife of William Penn.

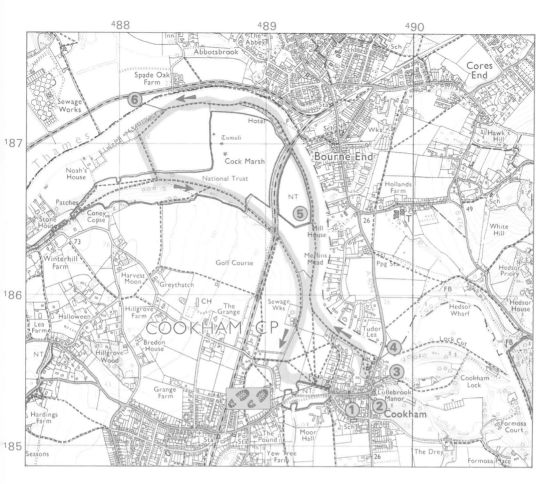

WALK 13

COOKHAM

A visit to a church made famous by painter Stanley Spencer is followed by a walk along the Thames towpath to Cock Marsh lying beneath an impressive chalk hill. Half way round there is an isolated pub where customers arrive by ferry.

ROUTE DIRECTIONS

4 miles. Allow 2 hours.
Start from Cookham Moor car park (grid ref: SU894853).

Follow the National Trust Cock Marsh signpost but keep ahead at The Crown to continue down the High Street ① to the Stanley Spencer Gallery ②.

Go left round the corner to pass the Tarry Stone ③.

Bear left by the timber-framed cottages to enter the churchyard ④. Take the left-hand path, passing the church tower, and go through a kissing-gate to reach the Thames.

Turn upstream on the towpath and go through the sailing club gates. At a stile the path enters Cock Marsh ⑤. Keep by the river and go through a gate to pass under the railway bridge. Soon the path passes The Bounty Inn and goes through two more riverside gates.

At Ferry Cottage ⑥ the path bears away from the water. Turn left at a path junction on to a wide path running south towards the steep hill. Go over the stile and turn left.

At a stile keep forward through a field and walk under the railway. There is another stile to cross before continuing in the same direction. The path rises to reach a golf course. Here go ahead on the parallel green lane by going down the steps next to the seat, where a post is waymarked 'permitted path'.

At the far end of the path climb over a stile into a field and bear round to the left to find a hidden stile. A short path leads into Cookham Moor car park.

POINTS OF INTEREST

① Cookham ceased to be on a main road in the 13th century when nearby Maidenhead Bridge was built. The erection of Cookham Bridge and the arrival of the railway within a few years of each other in Victoria's reign gave rise to commuting. The High Street has changed little since then although the buildings have new uses – the Old Forge is a restaurant. Also in the main street is Ovey's Farm which was a working farm when painted by Stanley Spencer.

② Painter Stanley Spencer has made Cookham famous. He was born one of nine children at Fernlea in the High Street (marked by a blue plaque) and set many of his religious paintings in the village. Christ is depicted being baptised at the Odney Club swimming pool, preaching outside the Harvester Ferry Inn and being crucified in the High Street as known villagers look on.

③ On the corner of Odney Lane is the mysterious Tarry Stone which has served as a boundary stone and a meeting place for centuries.

④ The newest part of the church is its Tudor tower which was added to the 12th-century nave. To the left of the high altar is the tomb of Robert Pecke, Henry VI's Master Clerk of the Spicery. The churchyard, which Spencer called 'that holy suburb of heaven', features in his *Resurrection, Cookham*, where the dead emerge from the tilting tombstones.

⑤ The 132-acre Cock Marsh is the finest marshy grassland in the National Trust's care. Rare wetland plants thrive here and breeding birds include redshank and lapwing. The marsh, grazed but free from agricultural improvements, has several Bronze Age burial mounds.

⑥ Ferry Cottage is a reminder that Spade Oak Ferry operated here until 1962, enabling towing horses and walkers to reach the towpath's continuation on the far bank.

WALK 14

HAMBLEDEN

A visit to a delightful, unspoiled brick-and-flint village nestling in a small valley just north of the River Thames. This waymarked route follows fields through the valley bottom and then makes an easy 363ft climb on to the Chiltern Hills, giving occasional distant views of the Thames. There is one short, stiff climb before reaching Hambleden.

ROUTE DIRECTIONS

5½ miles. Allow 2 hours.
Start from Hambleden village car park (grid ref: SU785866).

Walk through the churchyard, keeping the church on your right ①. At the lane turn right. Continue to a footpath sign and kissing-gate and follow a path towards some cottages. Just before reaching the cottages, turn left and walk parallel to the lane on your right through several fields and some houses, ignoring a cross-path.

About 50yds after entering a field in which the hedge is on your immediate left, turn left over a stile and walk diagonally towards a house. Cross a ladder-stile hidden in the hedge and continue to a lane. Turn left, then right at a T-junction, and continue to a footpath sign beside a farm drive. Take the path that climbs steadily up the hill and enters Cadmoor Wood to reach

a lane opposite a winery ②.

Turn left at the lane and in 770yds reach a footpath sign on the left and follow a path that runs through woods and emerges into a field. Turn right, keeping the field edge on your right, and walk to a stile in the corner of the field, then continue in the same direction to a sunken cross-path.

Turn left and follow a well-defined bridleway to a junction of paths at the bottom of a steep-sided valley. Turn right and follow a broad track for 1¼ miles ③. Turn left along an enclosed bridleway just beyond some estate cottages. After 660yds turn left along a waymarked cross-path that climbs steeply until dropping down to Hambleden ④.

POINTS OF INTEREST

① The church, originally Norman, has been much restored but contains a fine 17th-century monument to the d'Oyley family and an altar made from an oak carving that was once part of Cardinal Wolsey's bedhead.
② Luxters Farm now markets the well-known Hambleden Valley English Country Ale and Chiltern Valley Estate Bottled English Wine.
③ This is a typical Chiltern dry valley carved by a stream that has long since disappeared. The hills are covered in managed woodland, mostly beech, and the valley bottom is pasture.
④ The handsome flint Manor House, visible through the trees on the east side of Hambleden, was the home of W H Smith of bookshop fame and is still owned by the family. Many of the Victorian estate cottages in the village were built by him.

WALK 15

WHITELEAF HILL

The wooded slopes of the Chiltern Hills feature in this walk through some of Buckinghamshire's loveliest countryside where hamlets and history live peaceably together. Whiteleaf Hill lies on the Ridgeway path, which is a combination of the ancient Great Ridgeway and Icknield Way.

ROUTE DIRECTIONS

6 miles. Allow 3 hours.
Start from the car park at the summit of Whiteleaf Hill (grid ref: SP823036).

Walk to the far end of the car park and turn right along the Ridgeway Path (waymarked with an acorn). Continue to a wooden barrier that gives access to an open, grassy area ①. Turn right, and walk downhill through woods to a cross-path where you should leave the Ridgeway Path by turning right through the woods to descend steeply to a cross-track.

Continue in the same direction and take a wide track (the one with a stile) until it bears right and climbs steeply. At this point, turn left and follow a path that enters a wood and reaches a cross-path. Turn left then almost immediately right to follow a sunken path that emerges into a field. Follow the headland path through three fields and turn right through a gate that gives access to a metalled farm lane which descends to the road.

Cross the road and follow the farm road to Dirtywood Farm. Skirt the farm by taking the waymarked route around the left side and continue uphill and enter a wood. When the path emerges into a field, keep to the right-hand edge until reaching the top. Turn right through a gap and then left to keep the hedge on the left. Cross a stile into a wood and at a junction of paths continue in the same direction for a few yards until reaching a track. Turn right to reach a roughly metalled lane.

Turn right along the lane and walk past the Rising

Sun at Little Hampden ②. Just beyond the pub, turn right at a footpath sign and follow a driveway that leads to two houses. Just beyond The Croft follow a narrow, enclosed path that emerges at a large field. Cross the field towards a wood. Just before reaching the wood, turn left and follow the field edge to Warren Wood. Turn left along the field edge for 20yds, then turn right, enter the wood and follow a waymarked path, ignoring a path that shortly turns off to the left. On reaching a field, turn right, walk to the road, cross over and follow the field edge to another road.

Cross this road to a stile beside a gate, walk towards the stile visible on the skyline, and then aim for a stile just to the left of an estate cottage. Turn right and follow the drive past the church and Hampden House ③ and enter a broad track lined with trees that leads to a field. Bear slightly right, then follow the field edge, ignoring the track that turns off to the right. In 50yds the footpath crosses a stile and runs parallel to the bridleway ④.

Continue for a mile, ignoring all paths that cross or turn off the main route, until the path emerges from the wood and runs between a field and a tall hedge. Continue to a hut beside a radio mast. Turn sharp right through a hunting gate and follow the edge of the wood, ignoring all paths that turn off. In 220yds turn sharp left to continue just inside the wood until reaching an escarpment. Turn left and follow the Ridgeway Path to the car park.

POINTS OF INTEREST

① This viewpoint is actually a Neolithic tumulus. Immediately below, although not visible from here, is Whiteleaf Cross, whose age is thought to be medieval.
② Little Hampden is a charming hamlet with a church, a pub and a handful of houses.
③ Hampden House (now a school) was the home of democrat John Hampden who fought for the Parliamentary Army and died after the Battle of Chalgrove. He is buried in the churchyard opposite the house.
④ The hollow along which the footpath runs is part of the earthwork known as Grim's Ditch. Its origin is uncertain, but it probably dates from the Iron Age.

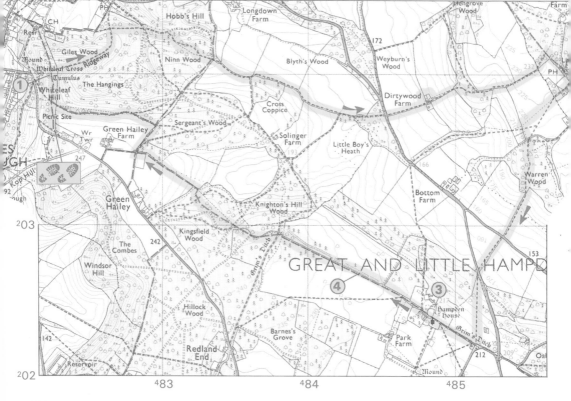

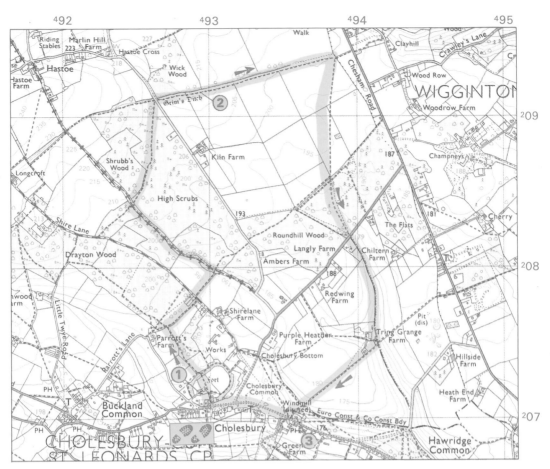

WALK 16
CHOLESBURY FORT

This easy, level walk in the Chilterns follows well-defined, waymarked paths through fields and woods, taking in two sites dating back to the Iron Age.

▲ Cholesbury church within the Iron Age fort

ROUTE DIRECTIONS

4½ miles. Allow 2 hours.
Start from Cholesbury Common where cars may be parked (grid ref: SP933071).

From the common, walk along the road towards the centre of Cholesbury and turn right along a footpath that runs beside the village hall. Continue in the same direction across fields and woodland ① until opposite the white, tile-hung Parrott's Farm surrounded by paddocks which can be seen through the hedge on the left. Cross the stile into the wood, turn right and walk to a lane.
   Turn left, and almost immediately right over a stile, and walk along the headland to High Scrubs Wood. Turn left inside the wood and follow the bridleway to a cross-path at a point just before the bridleway emerges from the wood. Turn right and walk to a lane.
   Cross the lane, enter a narrow strip of woodland ② and continue for ¾ mile until reaching a hedge at right angles to the path. Turn right and in 25yds reach a stile on your left. Do not cross the stile, but take the path that runs diagonally right across two fields to a wood. Enter the wood and turn right along a broad path for a few yards, then turn left along a narrow path that joins a wider path. Turn right and walk to the road.
   Cross the road and follow the farm lane to just pass Tring Grange Farm. Turn right over a stile and walk up the right-hand headland and then descend to

Cholesbury Common. Turn right for a few yards and then left along a path that runs to the edge of the common opposite the public house and windmill ③.

POINTS OF INTEREST

① Just beyond the village hall the route crosses the Iron Age earthwork of Cholesbury Fort. The parish church which can be glimpsed on the left was built inside the fort and it is an interesting example of the continuity of use of ancient sites (it is said that Saxons were baptised in the pond before the church was built). It was originally erected in the 13th century, but dismantled and rebuilt using the original materials in 1872.
② The bank and hollow form part of Grim's Ditch which may be seen in several places in the Chilterns. Archaeologists date it from the Iron Age, but are uncertain of its purpose. It may mark a boundary or even be the enclosing walls of a large ranch, but it was not thought to have been designed for defensive purposes.
③ The windmill, originally a smock mill, was built in 1863. In 1884 it was rebuilt as a tower mill using the original cap and fantail, but now it is a private house.

117

ACKNOWLEDGEMENTS

The Automobile Association wishes to thank the following libraries and
photographers for their assistance in the preparation of this book.

Doc Row 40 Swans, Swan Marking
The Mansell Collection 14 Easter Monday, 20 Elizabeth I, 20/21 Charles Dickens, 21 Disraeli, 22
Churchill, 22 Stanley Spencer, 23 Claude Duval, 25 Mail Coach, 46 Hop Picking, 71 Sir Francis Dashwood
Andy Williams Photo Library Cover Buckland

All remaining pictures are held in the Association's own library (AA Photo Library) with contributions
from: M Adleman, P Baker, M Birkitt, D Forss, A Grierly, S & O Mathews, D Noble, B Smith, R Surman,
M Trelawny, R Victor, W Voysey, P Wilson, T Woodcock

Ordnance Survey Maps covering the London Area

Routemaster and Routeplanner Maps

London is covered by Routemaster Map 9, South East England, which shows all the
motorways and main routes into London. Alternatively use the Great Britain Routeplanner
Map which covers the whole country on one map sheet.

Exploring with Landranger and Central London Maps

Landranger Series
$1\frac{1}{4}$ inches to 1 mile or 1:50,000 scale.
These maps cover the whole of Britain and are
good for local motoring and walking. Each
contains tourist information such as parking,
picnic places, viewpoints and rights of way.
Sheets covering London and the surrounding
area are:

165 Aylesbury & Leighton Buzzard
166 Luton & Hertford
167 Chelmsford & Harlow
175 Reading & Windsor
176 West London
177 East London
178 The Thames Estuary
186 Aldershot & Guildford
187 Dorking, Reigate & Crawley

188 Maidstone & Weald of Kent

Central London Map
8 inches to 1 mile [1:7920 scale]
This map covers the central part of London from
Earl's Court to Spitalfields, and Regents Park to
South Lambeth. Special features include full
street index, London Bus information, River Bus
route and tourist attractions.

Other titles available in this series are:
Brecon Beacons; Channel Islands; Cornwall;
Cotswolds; Devon and Exmoor; East Anglia;
Forest of Dean and Wye Valley; Ireland; Isle of
Wight; Lake District; New Forest; Northumbria;
North York Moors; Peak District; Scottish
Highlands; Snowdonia; South Downs; Wessex;
Yorkshire Dales